IMMANUEL

Matthew McNaught has written for the *Guardian* Long Read and *n+1*. He lives in Southampton, where he works in mental health. He won the inaugural Fitzcarraldo Editions Essay Prize for *Immanuel,* his first book.

'Matthew McNaught is a strong and welcome new voice in essayism, clear-sighted and hugely empathetic. In this deeply affecting account of his own spiritual journey, he weaves in and out of the byways of religious belief once known as "enthusiasm", charting the body-shaking, mind-breaking experiences of friends and strangers alike. By turns cynical, doubtful, wounded and yearning, his words give astonishing shape to the space that only faith can fill.'
— Marina Benjamin, author of *Insomnia*

'"Empathy" is a popular critical buzzword, but Matthew McNaught's writing exemplifies the work of empathy at its most intense and, dare one say, sincere. Whether his subject is ordinary Syrians trapped by war or the fellow parishioners of his childhood church, ensnared by a false prophet, he always gives voice to the motives and emotions of those he writes about, mixed as they are and fraught with tragic consequence. McNaught is a sublime listener who knows how to put listening into words.'
— Marco Roth, author of *The Scientists*

'Matthew McNaught's *Immanuel* is a mesmerizing and compelling trip to the very edges of faith. The author explores the seductive pull of radical belief systems that can lead followers towards communal joy, transcendence, human folly and, at times, brutality. Through his journey as a member of an evangelical Christian community in his youth to an adulthood of questioning the more extreme manifestations of this community in Nigeria, McNaught has created an expansive narrative that asks the fundamental questions around our need for faith and belonging whilst exploring their limits. *Immanuel* is a beautiful and important book.'
— Joanna Pocock, author of *Surrender*

Fitzcarraldo Editions

IMMANUEL

MATTHEW MCNAUGHT

CONTENTS

PREFACE

Immanuel was the sound of around a hundred people singing more or less in tune. It was baptisms in the River Itchen, picnics on the South Downs, praying in tongues in suburban living rooms.

Hebrew for 'God with us', Immanuel was a name uttered by the Prophet Isaiah, whose words were later recalled in Matthew's gospel as evidence of Christ's divinity: 'Behold, the virgin will be with child and will give birth to a son, and she will call Him Immanuel.' A bridge between the Old Testament and the New, Immanuel was God's promise to His people, fulfilled.

Immanuel was a house church first, before expanding to fill a rented room in Winchester Guildhall and then the grand Georgian building that stood on the opposite side of the Broadway. Immanuel was the centre of the world once. Long after it imploded, its gravitational pull remains.

When friends visit me in Southampton, I soon run out of things in the city to show them, so I take them on the 30-minute train ride to Winchester. We walk down the paved High Street, passing cafés and boutiques, turn right at the Buttercross into the Cathedral grounds, then head towards the Water Meadows. I always feel, as we set out on this tourist walk, a tug towards the Broadway at the bottom end of town.

When I visit Winchester alone, I'm more likely to submit to it. I stand on the pavement of the Broadway, the statue of King Alfred behind me, and look up at St John's House. The narrow lattice windows of the medieval undercroft. The broader windows of the assembly room above, and the painted ones of the non-existent third floor. I look for the paint pot and brushes on one of the windows of the top row, the trompe l'œil left in the nineties by Immanuel's resident painter-decorator, along with his name on the pot: 'Dave'. St John's is closed to the public now. I walk away with my longing unfulfilled.

I was happy to learn that there was a name for this kind of place – one that captures the strange charge it possesses. A hierophany, according to the religious scholar Mircea Eliade, is a point where the membrane between the sacred and the mundane world seems at its thinnest, where the divine feels within closest reach. Some hierophanies are built structures: altars, temples, obelisks. Some are portable, like the prayer pole of a wandering tribe. Some are offered up by the natural world: the ancient oak, the mountain top. It might have some inherent quality of awe or beauty. It might be improvised or arbitrary. What matters is that people come together around these points; shared rituals and stories accumulate. The moment I came across the word, the places of a church childhood came to mind. The stone floor of the undercroft. The light green carpet of the assembly room.

These were spaces in which we gathered as a single body and called on God. For the most part, He eluded me. I spent far more time in church feeling frustrated, bored or out of place than I ever did giving full-hearted praise. The question of how He moved, and of what precisely He promised, would divide and scatter us. Some of us – myself included – would lose our faith altogether. Others would end up on the extreme fringes of evangelical Christianity. Yet division is not the feeling first evoked when I think of my hierophanies. Instead there is a sense – visceral, undiminished by the passing of time – of being part of this body which extended beyond me.

Other things bring on this feeling. Only YouTube

knows about my late-night weakness for the old praise and worship songs that take me back to the assembly room. *Lord, you have my heart. And I will search for yours. Jesus, take my life and lead me on.* And meeting old church friends always feels different from, say, meeting friends from school. I ask after their families, and their names – 'How's Phil?' 'What's Anna doing these days?' – work a kind of spell that brings Immanuel fleetingly to life again.

I. EVERYONE NEEDS TO BE DELIVERED

In the video, TB Joshua walked along the front row, pressing the palm of his hand against each forehead he passed. A line of people collapsed in his wake, a cascade of Sunday dresses, football shirts, colourful West African fabrics. One woman cried out to him as he passed, her hands held up in supplication: 'The devil is using the Bible to torment me!' TB Joshua stopped. 'How does the devil use the Bible?'

She took a dog-eared Bible from under her arm, and explained how she was compelled to consult the book before doing anything. She couldn't cook, wash dishes or go out without its say-so. The woman was in her forties, hair tied back in a sensible ponytail, face taut with worry. 'I have destroyed six Bibles by doing this,' she said. Her husband stood beside her, looking down with a pained half-smile.

TB Joshua asked her to demonstrate how it worked. A leather handbag and a black shoulder bag were brought out and placed before her. 'Here are two bags now,' said TB Joshua. 'You don't know which one to carry, so ask!'

'I'd pray,' she said. 'Oh Lord, open my eyes! Which bag should I carry?' She opened her Bible at random. Her finger alighted on a passage. 'His glory is like the firstling of his bullock,' she read. 'And his horns are like the horns of unicorns.' She pointed to the leather handbag. 'Then I would know, because...'

TB Joshua cut her off. 'What does that say about this bag?' A ripple of laughter from the congregation. The woman seemed exasperated by the question. 'It says *positive* concerning this bag.'

He asked her to demonstrate going out. She put the Bible in the handbag and mimed a walk in her neighbourhood. The camera moved back as she made her way down the front row, stopping at imagined junctions to ask the Bible which way to go. Behind, TB Joshua looked on with a beatific smile, one arm folded across his chest, the other holding the microphone. Beyond him, a sea of congregants watched expectantly. Above them, the balconies, the mounted lights, the giant LED screens of the main auditorium of the Synagogue Church of All Nations, Lagos.

TB Joshua first entered my awareness as a curiosity: a sharp-suited, goatee-bearded Nigerian preacher on the chunky plastic cover of a VHS tape, which sat among books and audio-cassettes on the table at the back of the assembly room. It was the late nineties and I was in my teens. When I first watched the clips of his healings and exorcisms – which seemed to combine Billy Graham's stadium evangelism with the kinetic drama of WWE wrestling – they provoked, above all, my burgeoning teenage scepticism. There was also a faint hope, a question hovering: what if this was the real deal? It was the remnant of a familiar anticipatory wonder that soon evaporated entirely. In the years that followed, my aversion to TB Joshua deepened and intensified. He came to personify the toxic, tyrannical potential of the Born Again Christianity I'd left behind. After I started writing about Joshua, and the confluence of forces that connected him with the church of my childhood, a kind of wonder returned. Not at the possibility of his anointing, but at his audacity, and the sheer unlikeliness of what he had achieved.

It's hard to disentangle the facts of Joshua's life from his self-mythologising. The official SCOAN narrative is repeated in many online articles: his birth was foretold by a prophet, he spent fifteen months in his mother's womb, he received a divine revelation in 1987 while fasting for forty days and forty nights in an area of swampland that would later be called Prayer Mountain.

The basic facts are remarkable enough. Joshua was born into poverty in 1963, in a village called Arigidi in Ondo State, south-west Nigeria. He moved to Lagos as a young man, his secondary school education unfinished, and found work on a poultry farm. He was in his mid-20s when he founded his church. The earliest videos of SCOAN show a skinny young man addressing a small congregation under a bamboo tent, wearing a white gown and a long, ragged beard. He barely resembles the plump-faced, well-groomed millionaire pastor he would become, but his movements are unmistakable: the antic energy, the easy mastery of the crowd.

By the time he was fifty, TB Joshua had become a household name across much of Sub-Saharan Africa, and a Christian celebrity in many countries beyond. His satellite channel Emmanuel TV broadcast services and news of his philanthropy across several continents. His prophecies of world events gained tens of thousands of views on YouTube. He travelled the world, drawing vast crowds to his touring prayer events, known as crusades, in Africa, Asia, and Latin America. His church became a site of mass pilgrimage, unrivalled in Nigeria, receiving tens of thousands of visitors each week, many seeking healing or deliverance from demons. TB Joshua's fame transformed the Lagos neighbourhood of Ikotun-Egbe into a thriving commercial hub, as markets, banks, hotels and restaurants rose up to meet the demand of visitors.

'If I am going to the market,' the woman told TB Joshua, 'and I want to buy ogbono, and two people are selling ogbono...' She stopped in front of two women in the front row, pointing to one of them. 'I would ask, should I buy ogbono from this woman?'

She hunched over the bag hanging from her shoulder, opened the Bible inside and read haltingly: 'And Amon had a friend and his name was Jonathan, the son of David's brother, and Jonathan was a subtle man...' She looked up. 'Because it said that Jonathan was a subtle man, then I should not buy from this woman, because...' Drowned out by a surge of laughter from the crowd, she struck the air in frustration. TB Joshua spoke. 'From what you read now, there is nothing to show whether you should buy or not buy!'

'I read that Jonathan is a *subtle* man,' she said. 'That is somebody who is too crafty.'

TB Joshua asked how this problem affected her life. She said that she had narrowly avoided being hit by traffic while reading; that she had to consult the Bible if her husband wanted the two of them to meet as 'husband and wife'; that he got upset because it tended to say no.

TB Joshua doubled up with a laughter that spread through the congregation. Moments later, he turned serious. He faced the woman from a few metres away. 'How did this start?' he asked. She explained how it began ten years ago when a colleague showed her how to use the Bible to make decisions. 'It was working for me,' she said. 'But I was not doing it often.'

'Before,' said TB Joshua, 'it was working for you?'

'It is still working for me,' she said.

'Okay, it is still working for you,' he said.

'Why do you want to disconnect yourself?'

'Because it is a torment,' she said. 'People see me behaving abnormally, walking up and down the yard with the Bible. I do not even hide it anymore. I want to preach the Gospel. But not this way.'

The congregation laughed again, but the woman looked desperate.

'So something that worked for you,' said TB Joshua, 'is now tormenting you.'

She told him about the voice in her head that spoke constantly of death. 'That's why I carry the Bible,' she said. 'When I want to do something, the voice would be telling me that I would die or another person would die.'

'When you sleep, is there a strange man who normally comes to you?'

'Yes, sir.'

'And you know that you don't have affection for your husband...'

'You are very correct, sir.'

TB Joshua told her that she had a spiritual husband, a common form of demonic possession. From childhood, the woman had been betrothed to an evil spirit that now, since she'd married in the human realm, was determined to attack her and undermine her relationship. 'Don't let it surprise you that someone could use the Bible like this,' he said. Evil spirits, he explained, would use whatever was available. He held up his hand to exorcize the spirit. On the video, a man narrated as the woman fell to the ground.

I recognized the voice immediately. The sonorous English accent; the slight thespian flair. 'Having explained that all the lady needed was a thorough deliverance,' he said, 'Prophet TB Joshua prays for her in the name of Jesus Christ, delivering her in the power of the Holy Spirit.'

It was Eliot. He was two or three years younger than me – probably in his late twenties now. I imagined him in the editing booth in Lagos, watching the footage, writing the script for the voiceover.

I started watching Emmanuel TV on YouTube in around 2012. I watched the videos to hear these voices, to catch glimpses of the lives of my old church friends. A group of people from Immanuel became followers of TB Joshua in the early 2000s. As I moved away from the evangelical Christianity of my youth, they had pursued it to Lagos.

Dan Winfield was the first of my church friends to become a disciple. The oldest child of Gavin and Susan Winfield, he was nineteen when he went out in 2001, turning down a place on a university course in London. In 2006, he married Kate, a South African disciple. In the years after his arrival, his two sisters and brother joined him as disciples. Like the Winfield siblings, Eliot went out when he was in his late teens.

Immanuel was not the only British church to encourage its members to go to SCOAN. A number of young British Christians became disciples of TB Joshua, coming from churches in Southampton, Sheffield, Devon, and London, to name a few. Like Immanuel, the churches were evangelical, largely white and middle-class, with a hunger for seeing God move in dramatic ways.

Once in SCOAN, disciples would gradually cut off contact with the outside world. They lived in dormitories alongside a community of disciples. The innermost circle consisted largely of Yoruba-speaking Nigerians. The others were international – largely from the UK, South Africa and the US, as well as mainland Europe, Latin America and Asia. Disciples worked long hours keeping the ministry going: organizing foreign tours, producing videos, welcoming visitors. They gave sermons and learned TB Joshua's teachings by heart, in training to become evangelists and prophets themselves. During services, they triaged the crowds of visitors in the prayer line: selecting people to be prayed for by the Prophet and his closest protégés, known as the Wise Men; praying themselves for those who remained.

Gavin and Susan Winfield never lived in Lagos full time, but were frequent visitors. From the beginning of Dan's discipleship, they supported the ministry from afar. They organized group trips to SCOAN from the UK, and later helped out with TB Joshua's humanitarian work and foreign tours. Soon after Dan got married, he was relocated to London with his wife to help set up a UK branch of SCOAN.

With time, friends and relatives of the Winchester disciples became alarmed at the extent of their devotion. Personalities appeared to change. On the rare visits home, disciples were odd and evasive in conversation, speaking of little other than TB Joshua, replying to questions with a patchwork of quotes from his teachings. Susan's sister and brother tracked down other former disciples, whose stories about life in SCOAN convinced them that their family had been drawn into a cult.

Much of this I gathered later. For most of the 2000s, SCOAN existed on the periphery of my awareness. My old church friends' devotion to TB Joshua was utterly alien to me: one of the weirder outcomes of an evangelical childhood that I was relieved to have left behind. It wasn't until 2010, after Dan and Kate Winfield left SCOAN suddenly, that I started paying more attention.

Watching Emmanuel TV, I would find the Winchester disciples interviewing visitors, asking about the problems that brought them to SCOAN, and the dramatic results of TB Joshua's prayer. I would see them giving sermons in the main auditorium, striding across the stage, micro-phone in hand, leading the crowd in call-and-response. What were the forces that kept them there? What did they see in TB Joshua? What, for that matter, did anyone see in him?

Few of the videos gave much in the way of an an-swer. Some were just boring. In TB Joshua's sermons, he seemed to take a banal Christian platitude and make it last half an hour. He'd repeat it, restate it, get the congregation to tell it to their neighbour. I'd skip forward a few minutes and he'd still be saying it. There were eloquent Nigerian pastors, I was sure, but TB Joshua was not one of them. Other videos I found abhorrent: the lines of people hold-ing placards naming their ailments – AIDS, CANCER, ARTHRITIS; the confidence with which TB Joshua moved down the row, raising his hands to heal each one.

Why did I keep coming back to the deliverances? Perhaps because watching them, I was not entirely im-mune to TB Joshua's charm. There was something powerful about the way he moved so deftly between play-fulness and sincerity. I could almost imagine being won over by him. The videos were also compelling because I couldn't figure out what was going on. Was I witnessing a meaningful cathartic ritual? A scene of exploitation or abuse? Or just one of cynical artifice? On the one hand, the YouTube thumbnails were pure clickbait: men with bulging eyeballs, young women with faces caught in quasi-orgasmic contortions; titles like 'WATCH ALL HELL BREAK LOOSE IN CHURCH!' or 'SATANIC SEDUCTION! NO MAN CAN RESIST MY BODY!' The demons shouted phrases that would turn up across multiple deliverances. Was this evidence of a script, or at least of preparation or prompting? The performanc-es were worthy of the Nollywood horror films produced down the road in Lagos. There was something addictive in the dependable rise and resolution of the story arc: the set-up, the conflict, and then the climax, in which the possessed person collapsed to the ground under the power of prayer. I was often moved, despite myself, by the final scene of the exorcisms. Lying on the floor, the recipients of prayer were commanded to stand up. It felt oddly voyeuristic to witness this moment, like catching someone waking up and remembering who they are. They'd open their eyes, adjust their clothes and gather themselves up, before rising, dazed and unburdened, to their feet. This was not pure fiction. It was clear that there was truth in these encounters.

The deliverances were an odd mixture of the chaotic and the formulaic. They were led either by TB Joshua or one of the Wise Men. When a possessed person came forward, the deliverer would always ask the same questions. They'd first demand that the demon identify itself. The demon, speaking through its host, would respond with a name. 'I am the Lion,' said one. 'I am Leviathan,' said another. 'I am the Queen of the Coast.' 'I am the Boss of the Boss.' 'I am the Serpent of Nembe Kingdom.'

The deliverer would ask how many demons or spirits were occupying the host. There was rarely just one. The demons usually shouted something vague: 'We are legion!' or 'We are numberless!' This kind of answer was rarely accepted. The deliverer would push for a specific number, as if driven by some obscure bureaucratic imperative. 'HOW MANY?' he would shout again and again, until the demon spokesperson finally gave in: 'There are seven of us.'

Another one said there were five. Another said they consisted of twenty-one elders, whose powers came from the rainbow colours of the seven seas. One man, dubbed King of the Wizards by TB Joshua, had been possessed by 186 evil spirits. He'd had 180 cast out already, but 6 were still hanging on. 'This guy is very dangerous,' TB Joshua warned the congregation.

The deliverer would ask the demon how they entered, how they operated, what they wanted. Interrogation over, he would raise his hand, strike the air and shout – 'OUT! IN THE MIGHTY NAME OF JESUS CHRIST!' The possessed person would be thrown back, screaming and convulsing. Some would vomit clear fluid into a pool on the tile floor. Some held out for longer than others, darting around the auditorium like trapped animals, before succumbing and falling to the ground. After they stood up and thanked Jesus Christ for their deliverance, the video would cut to an animated title screen: 'TESTIMONY TIME'. The newly delivered person appeared in a change of clothes and recounted their ordeal.

My old church friends. What does this even mean, when I have been churchless and agnostic for over fifteen years? The bond feels at once tenuous and profound. Gavin and Susan Winfield were, along with my parents, among the earliest members of the church. Like their children, I belonged to the sizeable first generation of native Immanuelites. We were raised together, in and out of each other's houses, sharing Sunday lunches and camping trips.

For a long time the Winfields were my favourite Immanuelite family to visit. They had the nicest garden. They had the best snacks – Gavin's speciality was millionaire shortbread, the height of decadence in the early 90s. The children lined up roughly in age with my siblings and me. Perhaps the biggest draw was their collection of

Christian rock music. It was at the Winfield's that I first encountered the rap-rock of DC Talk, the harmony-drenched indie rock of Jars of Clay. At an age when I was fast learning to be embarrassed by my tribe (the corduroys, the acoustic guitars, the brown-bread wholesomeness), the Winfields were emissaries of a Christian culture that was new, exciting, alive. Gavin and Susan had a modern people-carrier with a sliding door, which looked particularly sleek and space-age when parked alongside my parents' 1960s camper van. Once a month, on a Saturday night, a group of us Immanuel youth would pile into the back, and either Gavin or Susan would drive us to Southampton Community Church for a youth service called Cutting Edge, whose resident worship band would later find global fame as Delirious. The songs were epic, joyous, unashamedly Christian. The soaring singalong of 'Did You Feel the Mountains Tremble'. The folky stomp of the 'Happy Song'. The anthemic groove of 'History Maker'. The floor would quake with the po going. 'Is it true today,' we'd sing, over what was probably the best bassline in Christian music, 'that when people pray, cloudless skies will break, kings and queens will shake? Yes, it's true. And I believe it. I'm living for You.'

'People of God, we are listening to our sister,' said Michael to the congregation. 'We are learning a lot from what she is saying. This is someone who has *practical* experience. Someone who was part of that Kingdom.'

The video was entitled 'A MERMAID FROM HELL WASHES UP IN CHURCH!' The woman had been explaining how she'd been crowned Queen Mother of the Marine World; how she could cure infertility by sending snake spirits to enter the womb; how the baby would grow but the snake would kill the mother.

Conducting the interview at the front of the auditorium, Michael seemed at home with the subject matter, at ease with the crowd. In the years since he'd been at SCOAN, his accent had gained a Nigerian tinge. As the youngest of the Winfields, he'd been the last to go out. He'd become a disciple when he was 16; his parents had let him give up his A-levels.

'Our sister is explaining that in the spiritual kingdom of darkness, the Marine World had the power to give wealth,' said Michael. 'But conditions were attached.'

Watching the video, I was struck by the depth of Michael's immersion. I'd heard that disciples saw little of Nigeria outside of the SCOAN complex. But a lot of Nigeria came into SCOAN. He must have absorbed so much in his years as a disciple: the dialects, the culture, the local traditions and stories. What other white Brit knew as much as him about spiritual husbands and marine spirits?

The woman spoke at great length about the intricate workings of the Marine World, heading off on tangents, talking with such intensity that she barely paused for breath. Ten, fifteen, twenty minutes passed. This was not good TV. I imagined the congregation losing patience. I couldn't help feeling anxious on Michael's behalf. How would he wrap it up? He was unfazed. Far from curtailing her story, he pressed for more information.

'OK Madam, we want to take it step by step,' he said. 'Exactly *how* would you go about giving people wealth in this physical world?'

What was odd about these videos was how unchristian it all seemed. These lengthy accounts often seemed to be a mixture of traditional West African beliefs and individual confabulation. Their reality was always taken for granted. Every spiritual entity was regarded as demonic, but nothing was dismissed as superstition or fantasy. Why was so much airtime given to this amateur demonology? Why did we need to know our senior demons from our supervisor demons, our water spirits from our snake spirits, if Jesus Christ was going to be the answer anyway?

Later, I recalled how the gospels were full of exorcisms and sorcerers. In the Book of Acts, Paul curses a magician, striking him blind. Mary Magdalene was said to have been possessed by and delivered from demons. According to the Gospel of Luke, there were precisely seven of them. The world that Michael inhabited was a long way from suburban England. Perhaps it wasn't so far from the world of the New Testament.

'It started when I was seven,' said Rosemary, a woman from Ghana. 'I was half-naked, wearing a white cloth. I knelt behind my mum. A cow was killed. They poured the blood into a calabash. I dipped my middle finger in the blood and placed it on my tongue. That was how the covenant was made.'

The spirits in these videos fell broadly into two groups. There were those who were ancient inhabitants of the land. They were spirits of the forest and the water, taking the form of mermaids, snakes, crocodiles. They ruled over the mangrove swamps of the Nigerian Delta; the mountains, forests and rivers of the Ghanaian Volta. These spirits were often passed down from one generation to another. Sometimes this happened through a deliberate ritual, like Rosemary's covenant. Sometimes they were passed on inadvertently, like a hereditary disease.

Then there were the modern spirits. Untethered from the land or the bloodline, they occupied the untamed wilds of the internet and technology. A demon known as

Numeral lived in numbers and the letters of the alphabet, possessing people through passwords and ID codes. Others would lie in wait on a website like a computer virus, ready to enter anyone who opened the page. One man explained how he was possessed by a demon who inhabited a page on Facebook. He'd clicked on an image that appeared on his feed then scrolled through a series of pictures. It was then that the demon entered him. He held up print-outs of the images to the congregation: a red-skinned demon with giant horns, a picture of Gollum from *Lord of the Rings* wearing a dinner jacket.

In isolation, these testimonies were bizarre. Taken together, they seemed to tell a story of dislocation, of navigating the uncertainty of an ever-shifting, globalized world. The ways of the ancestors weren't working. And modernity, with all its technologies and diversions, was just as diabolical.

During Testimony Time, the interviewer would ask each person how their demons manifested. After all the florid detail of the spirit world, the outward symptoms of possession were surprisingly mundane: losing jobs, businesses failing, accidents, illnesses, miscarriages, trouble concentrating, marital discord, lashing out at kids. The demons were as strange to me as any fantasy novel, but here was something I understood only too well: the impulse to gather a crowd of sorrows and give them a name.

I watched exorcisms on YouTube at night. In the daytime, I made telephone calls. I spoke to plumbers from Hythe, military veterans from Gosport, HR managers from Chandler's Ford. I worked for an NHS psychological therapies service. Each person had made contact because they were depressed, anxious or otherwise in distress. Each time, I asked them the same list of questions on my assessment template and typed their answers. What's your main problem? When did it start? What are your physical symptoms, thoughts, feelings?

The service was part of a nationwide initiative aiming to make evidence-based therapy available to the masses for the first time in the UK. It was not without its critics. Some said that the Cognitive Behavioural Therapy (CBT) that formed the basis of our service offered a quick fix for complex problems. Others said that it expected low-paid practitioners with minimal qualifications to do work previously done by psychologists. Could you really teach people how to lead someone out of the depths of depression after just a year's training? As one of these low-paid, scantly qualified practitioners, it was in my interest to be optimistic.

As a Psychological Wellbeing Practitioner (PWP), my job was to assess new patients and then, along with my supervisor, decide on the most appropriate treatment. I'd take on the more straightforward cases, offering them up to eight sessions of CBT-based 'Guided Self Help' over the phone. I'd step up the more severe cases to a higher level of the service, or refer them out to specialist teams. What us PWPs lacked in training and experience, we more than made up for in questionnaires. We had a diagnostic questionnaire for everything. Panic Disorder, Social Anxiety Disorder, Post-Traumatic Stress Disorder, Obsessive Compulsive Disorder, Generalized Anxiety Disorder.

It wasn't always straightforward. In our supervisions with Senior PWPs, we'd have discussions about whether someone was depressed or just grieving, if someone had GAD or SAD; OCD, PTSD, BPD or all three. We were aware, of course, that none of us knew for sure. We were novices, as yet uninitiated in the complexities of the diagnostic model. All diagnoses we recorded were strictly provisional. Our role was not to understand the details, but to maintain the smooth running of the service: ushering people in, managing the most manageable, directing others to the right support.

The 45-minute assessment was packed with questions, a fraught compromise between the therapeutic impulse and the bureaucratic, and I nearly always overran. It was good to hear people's stories. For some people, there seemed to be a power in telling them, and in having them heard, even in this limited form. Several times, partway through assessments, people mentioned to me that they'd never talked to anyone about this stuff before. Some of those I worked with got better. More often than not, they didn't. If they didn't drop out, I'd step them up to step 3 for full-strength CBT. I liked the job, but I longed to ascend to that higher tier, to wield those strange acronyms with precision, to become a real therapist.

In the meantime, I learned the questionnaires off by heart. *Feeling down, depressed or hopeless. Feeling compelled to count while doing things. Having trouble concentrating. Feeling afraid as if something awful might happen.* We asked the questions, in part, so that our commissioners could know who had been delivered from which disorder. The electronic records system had added a feature that illustrated this on each patient's file. When someone who started with a high score dropped into the 'healthy' range, a tiny icon would appear: a little stickman with his arms raised above his head, backed by yellow rays that shot upwards and outwards in all directions like some kind of celestial light.

Some people struggled to complete the questionnaires at all. The last question on the PHQ-9 would ask each person to rate, on a scale of zero to three, how often in the last two weeks they'd had thoughts of being better off dead or wanting to harm themselves. 'I don't want to be dead, exactly,' someone would tell me, after a long pause. 'Too many people need me. But every day, I want it to be over. If I could just press a button and stop existing, I wouldn't hesitate.'

I'd make sympathetic noises into my headset. But the questionnaire would be filling my screen, waiting for the last box to be checked. 'I'm sorry,' I'd say, 'but I'm going to need a number.'

At some point, I took a break from my Emmanuel TV habit to watch some other Nigerian pastors on YouTube. SCOAN was not the biggest ministry in Lagos: several churches boasted more than double its 50,000 person capacity. There were more esteemed Nigerian pastors than TB Joshua. It seemed odd that out of all of them, it was TB Joshua who had the most appeal outside of West Africa and the diaspora, and who'd attracted a large following of foreign disciples who hung on his every word.

I watched Matthew Ashimolowo, from the London-based Kingsway International Christian Centre, who was about ten years older than Joshua. He had a similar kinetic energy, but with an added showbiz slickness. Rising to a full-throated growl in a US black gospel style – 'Can I get an AMEN!'– he threw out Bible verses and paraphrased the stories, his every sing-song line echoed by the jazzy noodling of a Hammond organ. I watched Paul Adefarasin, the pastor of House on the Rock, who had a barrel chest and film star looks, delivering a TED talk-like sermon to a hall of smart young professionals in an accent that shifted fluidly between American, Lagosian and upper-class English. I watched E. A. Adeboye of the Redeemed Christian Church of God, wearing a checked shirt and trousers like the 1970s maths professor that he used to be, speaking to a vast crowd in a lilting, avuncular baritone.

At first, it was hard to see what TB Joshua had on these guys. But I knew that the Immanuelites didn't go to Lagos for slickness, intellect or dignified gravitas. I remembered from Immanuel the power of an uneducated Man of God. Smith Wigglesworth was a big name in my youth: an illiterate Yorkshireman who became a world-renowned preacher and healer in the first half of the twentieth century, and whose transcribed and tidied-up teachings were evangelical bestsellers. The less literate the messenger, the assumption went, the more authentic the divine message must be. It was precisely TB Joshua's rough edges and humble background that appealed.

The arrangement seemed to be mutually beneficial. For all his fame, TB Joshua had been rejected by Nigeria's Christian establishment. Both the Christian Association of Nigeria and the Pentecostal Fellowship of Nigeria denied him admission, citing the unorthodox claims he made about himself (his insistence, for example, that he became a Christian while still in the womb, during his 15-month gestation). His white, middle-class Western disciples may have been drawn to SCOAN for its raw authenticity. But the prominence of their faces and voices on Emmanuel TV lent his ministry an air of international sophistication in the eyes of his supporters, making up for his outcast status among his fellow men of God.

Rosemary from Ghana explained how she took a trip to see a fetish priest. She asked if he could liberate her from the trouble caused by her spiritual husband, a merman from the Volta river. He said that the only way to appease the spirit was to make the marriage official.

Perhaps these testimonies began to explain the appeal of TB Joshua's brand of Christianity to his home crowd. It did not dismiss the spiritual entities of local tradition, but swallowed them whole, retaining their uncanny vitality, their rootedness in the terrain. TB Joshua avowed the existence of this phantasmagoria of snake spirits and mermen while superseding them in authority.

Rosemary described the wedding. It took place at midnight on the riverbank. She whispered her worries into the ear of a dove and let it fly away. In the distance, over the river, a light appeared. The fetish priest told her that this was her spiritual husband. The ceremony was complete. She would be free to live her own life, he promised, but for one night a week, she belonged to the merman. She followed the instructions, but soon her troubles multiplied. Again and again, the story was told in different ways. Futile attempts to defeat or appease the demons would lead to ever-greater entanglement, ever-escalating torment. It was dizzying after a while. I remembered the song of the old woman who swallowed the cat to catch the bird, having swallowed the bird to catch the spider, having swallowed the spider to catch the fly.

After the testimonies ended, TB Joshua would often address the crowd. His teaching was in the usual style. But in the wake of these convoluted stories of the spirit world, it worked on me in a different way. His speech was transformed, somehow, by the chaos that preceded it.

'What you wish to others,' he said in one video, 'God wishes to you.' He did a lap of the stage, smiling broadly, then stopped to say it again: 'What you wish to *others*...' – he swept his hand from the right to the left – '... God wishes to *you*.'

Teaching that could have been banal now brought a strange kind of relief. It had the weight and symmetry of wisdom, or at least felt momentarily like it might. It rung out like a struck bell, cleared the air, cut through the whole rat-king tangle.

In the final throes before being exorcized, many demons repeated the same phrase. 'HERE THERE IS LIGHT!' they'd shout, in tones of horror and rage. This, I realized, was the whole spectacle of deliverance: a move from obscurity to clarity; from that which was plural, chaotic, endlessly shapeshifting, to that which was singular, simple, eternal. Darkness and doubt were banished. Goodness prevailed.

'EVERYONE NEEDS TO BE DELIVERED' was the title of the first video in a YouTube playlist specializing in an obscure Emmanuel TV subgenre: the exorcisms of the Prophet TB Joshua's own disciples and followers. Several of my old church friends had their demons cast out. These scenes differed from the usual exorcisms. The performances were oddly stilted, lacking the manic spontaneity of the others. One or two disciples embodied the demons with theatrical gusto, but many seemed to submit to the ritual as an unpleasant obligation. It was hard to believe that any of them had volunteered for this. The videos were at once hard to watch and grimly compelling, like seeing a bad panto and a snuff film rolled into one.

Susan Winfield's demon sounded a lot like Susan. There was no satanic fury, no guttural roar, just a scolding Middle England staccato: the kind of voice that might, under different circumstances, demand to speak to the manager. 'Who are you?' the Wise Man asked. 'I am the Spirit of Death!' she said. 'From the mother's side, from the father's side... We have been here a long time!' Her husband Gavin looked on with a blank expression, awaiting his turn.

At one point, Susan-as-Demon did an awkward bit of product placement: taking a small bottle of TB Joshua's anointed water out of a pocket and throwing it on the ground, complaining about how it had shielded Susan from demonic attack. The anointed water was not for sale, but came as a free gift with certain TB Joshua-themed merchandise. Did Susan believe what she was saying? What was compelling her to say it?

There was something debasing about these scenes. Several of the disciples were asked how they were affected by the Spirit of Lust: another word, it seemed, for an average adult libido after years of being single and sleeping in a dorm.

'The Spirit of Lust is... a long time ago,' said a bearded, middle-aged Greek disciple. 'How do you operate in him?' the Wise Man repeated. He mumbled a reply then trailed off. 'SPEAK OUT!' said the Wise Man. The disciple stared at the ground. 'I have caused him to masturbate... Have sex in the dream... Going up and down with women...' he said. 'Before he came to this ministry...' he added.

The other times the disciples turned up on Emmanuel TV, they were oddly blank and inscrutable. Even when they delivered lengthy sermons, nothing of their own personalities came through. They channelled TB Joshua down to the last gesture. In the words of their demons, there was a hint of inner life.

'I saw a great star,' said another disciple-as-demon. 'I said this star can touch every continent. I saw it shining before he was born. I said this star will never manifest!' Variations on this line recurred in each disciple deliverance. They all traced out the same oscillation between greatness and wretchedness. Each disciple had an awesome destiny; there was no room to be good-hearted and historically insignificant. Each one was a pitiful failure, powerless against demonic attack. The disciple's greatness could only be fulfilled through the Man of God's intercession. 'The Prophet TB Joshua is protecting this boy!' protested the demon of a young South African disciple.

In Susan Winfield's exorcism, the Wise Man asked her demon what it had done to harm her. There was a story of a car crash, a plot against Susan's life which she'd miraculously survived. Then it spoke of Susan's children. Dan, her oldest son, had recently left SCOAN with his wife after a decade as a disciple.

'They are promised children,' Susan-as-Demon said. 'Each one of them was given a name that they would serve God. But I, the Spirit of Death, I do not like it!' She jabbed a finger at the Wise Man. 'I want to take them out. I'm *going* to take them out. I've already started!'

¶ Pastor Graham stands by the edge of the River Itchen and addresses the crowd. He is tall and slim, wearing linen trousers and a woollen jumper, holding a song sheet in his raised right hand. Tony, our worship leader, stands next to him with an acoustic guitar. The rest of us are spread out in a wide arc on the riverbank, the adults standing on the grass in overcoats and cardigans, a few of us kids sitting on the stones of the rockery by the footbridge. Behind us, the red-brick terraced houses of Water Lane, Winchester.

I'd got an invitation to join a Facebook group called Ex-Immanuelites. It was 2010, and our former church administrator had scanned and uploaded a bunch of old photos. Tag anyone I've missed, he wrote. Over the following years, he would occasionally upload another batch.

It isn't clear whose baptism the photo is from. Moments later, he or she would come forward from the crowd and head down into the river along with two other church members. The three of them would wade out through the cold, clear water, navigating a path around rocks and the odd beer can. The baptisee would be lowered back against the river's flow, emerging reborn to cheers and applause. On the riverbank, someone would be waiting with a bath-towel, someone with a flask of tea.

The photos spanned over twenty years. There were Bible Weeks, weddings, New Forest outings, Kids' Club fancy dress parties. In the comments sections, people reminisced and tagged other ex-Immanuelites. The photos were already artefacts of a distant past. The comments were casually wistful, but there was a darkness – unacknowledged, but surely felt by all – in the story that the photos told.

'Dear Friends,

We apologize that our email earlier this week came as a shock to many. Since then, many have been asking why we made such a drastic decision after ten years of total commitment to SCOAN. We pray that as you read, you will examine all we say in the light of God's Word. It's so important to have independent minds – to go to God to seek for the truth.'

Dan and Kate Winfield sent the email to a group of SCOAN friends in 2010, but it travelled further than they expected. A number of Dan's former Immanuel friends were forwarded the email, one of whom forwarded it to me.

'First of all we would like to sincerely apologize for misleading you... We kept silent about many things that take place at SCOAN in Lagos. We have also misled you by justifying and making excuses for many inexcusable things... No matter our good intentions, before God we are responsible for this, and therefore ask for your forgiveness.

Over the last few years, Kate has suffered with depression. She made sure she was strong for the team and in public, but it was a continual battle. In private, she would say things like, "I wish I was never born," or "I'm praying for God to kill me." Last week, things became really bad and I sat her down in desperation to try and find out what was happening. On the outside her behaviour didn't make sense. My parents paid for a nice flat for us, we had a beautiful child, a great team and a growing church. She eventually broke down and explained that, over the course of several years, TB Joshua had been summoning her to his room and sexually abusing her. He told her that he was doing these things to help her with her spiritual problems. These occasions took place between 2001 and

2005. She felt that talking about this would betray TB Joshua and God. But within her, she could not forgive herself and felt that God could not forgive her. As a former disciple of TB Joshua I fully understand. As disciples we are conditioned to consider TB Joshua as infallible. Disciples will say he has weaknesses, but no disciple will tell you a weakness that he has. We basically consider him above correction. We justify everything he does. Anyone who speaks against him is labelled as a Blasphemer.'

The email gave a long list of the violence and cruelty they'd witnessed over the years at SCOAN: 'TB Joshua whipping disciples until they bled and urinated on the floor, making disciples kneel for three days as a form of punishment.'

'In the few days after Kate told me,' Dan continued, 'it was like a veil was removed from my eyes. I realized that although I have seen wonderful miracles at SCOAN and received some great messages from TB Joshua, at the end of the day he is not perfect and is just a man.'

When my wife and I first visited Dan and Kate at their house in Bristol, I was a little nervous. I imagined that an afternoon with survivors of an abusive cult could only be intense. They greeted us, introduced us to the kids – they'd recently had a second child – and put the kettle on. It was like meeting with old friends. Talking to Dan, I felt the familiarity borne out of old bonds, but without the inhibitions of the Immanuel days. Kate, too, with her wit and irreverence, her ease and intimacy with Dan, left me feeling like I'd known her for years.

We talked a bit about SCOAN. They told us that they now had little contact with Dan's parents and siblings, who remained devoted to TB Joshua, and had rejected Dan and Kate's accusations as lies. Dan and I reminisced a little about Immanuel. Mostly we talked about every-thing other than church: life with kids, Dan's new role in a tech start-up, and the state of the world. Among the toys and picture books, there were stacks of *Economist* magazines, books on business and current affairs. If any-thing betrayed their years of single-minded devotion to TB Joshua, it was the keenness with which they now engaged with the wider world, as if making up for lost time.

I was surprised to learn that before Dan became a disciple, he'd been due to start a degree in development studies at SOAS in London; he'd ended up turning it down in favour of SCOAN. I'd done the same degree at Leeds: a mixture of politics and economics with a focus on the post-colonial world. Like him, I'd also gone to live abroad, moving to Damascus after graduation, where I taught English and studied Arabic. Why did I move there? When asked the question, I'd give one of several answers. None were untrue, but neither were they entire-ly convincing to me. I went to Damascus, I think, because I wanted to be the kind of person who did that kind of thing. Walking to work in my early twenties, I'd often fan-tasize about speaking Arabic fluently: sitting with Middle Eastern men in some sheesha café, an exotic glossolalia leaving my lips. Besides the specific fascinations of the region, what I shared with Dan was a sense of what I was rejecting: a staid, conventional life of marriage, mort-gages and graduate schemes. Living a life of vitality, we believed, required getting far away from Winchester. Now, like him, I was back in England, wishing I'd started saving for a deposit sooner.

The meeting left me even more puzzled than before. Reconnecting with Dan made me feel more acutely the longing for Immanuel church that had been gradually growing in me as I got older. At the same time, to know Dan and Kate's story was to confront the catastrophic endpoint of the worldview of our youth. Dan was clear that the path that took him to SCOAN had started in Immanuel.

I couldn't square up Dan and Kate's intelligence in person – and the moral clarity displayed in their email – with the abundance of awful and bizarre things that they'd witnessed and tolerated in Lagos. What kept them there for so long? I knew, at least, that it was not for want of brains or integrity that they were drawn into SCOAN. Their exit from the church led me to reconnect with old friends from Immanuel with whom I'd previously lost touch. We were now joined in dismay. I spoke to friends from the youth group, and several of the older generation of Immanuelites. I had long discussions with my parents and siblings. My older brother and I set up a blog called TB Joshua Watch, to which several church friends contributed. It was almost impossible, we discovered, to find credible information about SCOAN online. The negative articles were as hyperbolic as the puff pieces: he was either a great Man of God or the Antichrist. We started the blog as a way to gather the few critical accounts of TB Joshua scattered around the internet.

During the conversations with ex-Immanuelites, we spoke as much about Immanuel as SCOAN. We revisited, in the light of Dan's revelations, our shared history. One friend lent me her mum's stash of church magazines, which I read compulsively, as if looking for clues.

What had happened to us? Why had so many Immanuelites, and so many other British evangelicals, been taken in? Across these conversations, one word kept coming up: *revival*.

For a few years, starting in the mid-1990s, the word possessed an electric, heart-quickening charge. 'Today, respected prophets and church leaders at home and abroad are confidently predicting that "the Lord will surely give us the land" in revival,' wrote our pastor Graham in the Summer 1996 issue of the church magazine.

Revival, we learned, would be a tidal wave, an all-consuming fire. In cities, crowds of non-believers would fall down in the streets, floored by the Holy Spirit. Churches would be flooded with people, convicted of sin, desperate to give their lives to Christ. Life would never be the same again.

The prophecies rang true. Things were already happening. The church was expanding; we'd moved into St John's House and were gaining new members each month. Us first generation natives were moving into our teens, restless and hungry, excited by the prospect of a move of God that would shake up the complacency of the established church. For me, revival also meant certainty. I was privately struggling with growing doubts. If the prophecies came true, God's presence and power would be undeniable.

We heard about great moves of God elsewhere. Some Immanuelites went out to see for themselves, coming back with reports of great signs and wonders in Buenos Aires, Pensacola, Toronto. At the Toronto Airport Christian Fellowship, the Holy Spirit was said to be manifesting in strange and dramatic ways. People were collapsing, convulsing, weeping, laughing uncontrollably, slurring as if drunk. This phenomenon, known as the Toronto Blessing, spread around the world. Soon it was happening in Immanuel. Worship became more intense and emotional than it had ever been. We had evening meetings that lasted long into the night. I remember the mixed excitement and frustration of these days; excitement that something extraordinary seemed to be happening; frustration that it seemed to be happening to everyone but me.

It feels right to recount the history of Immanuel using 'we'. But soon in the story, the pronoun starts to break up. Some Immanuelites quietly believed that the Toronto Blessing was not of God but of Satan. Others saw it as pure hype, a sort of mass hysteria. My own parents had been unimpressed by this sort of thing since someone was slain in the spirit at a prayer meeting in our living room, breaking a new storage unit that they'd saved up for. For many others, it was divine, life-changing, the first ripples of a far greater wave to come.

'Perhaps you, like us, will look back on this past year with thankfulness and disappointment, with joy and sorrow.' Thus began the New Year editorial in the first church magazine of 1998, written by Pastor Graham. 'We are thankful for the many answered prayers and the start of new faith adventures that have been birthed in Immanuel church over the year; disappointed that revival seems slow in coming. We have joy in friendships established and sorrow in others that have been lost or damaged...'

In early 1997, a visiting preacher had put a date on the coming revival. I think it was a day in May. It came and went. The people in the supermarkets and betting shops of Winchester remained vertical and unrepentant.

Dan Winfield had reminded me, during our visit to Bristol, of the courtesy drop. This is when, after failing to be slain in the spirit despite being prayed for at length, you politely fall to the ground anyway. It was a manoeuvre I knew well. The evangelical equivalent of faking an orgasm, it hurried the encounter through to its conclusion, sparing both of you the embarrassment of an anticlimax. It also dug you one inch deeper into the pit of your own inadequacy: not just a failure, but a fake.

I hadn't realized that the move was common enough to have a name. I'd never spoken about it with anyone before. I was also struck that Dan, whom I'd envied in my mid-teens for his passion and spiritual receptivity, had been racked with the same guilt and doubt as me. That bi-polar lurch between fervour and frustration was more common than I'd thought.

'Let us start this year' continued Graham in his '98 editorial, 'with renewed determination to persevere together to see "His Kingdom come and His will be done on earth as it is in Heaven." Remember the challenge from Gerald Coates: "If you *can* live without revival, you *will* live without revival."' We faced either revival or failure; wretchedness or world-shaking awesomeness. And if revival didn't come, it was because we – or some of us – didn't want it enough.

One side effect of believing for an imminent miracle is that you have to account for its absence. Believing we were destined to be a vanguard in an awesome move of God entailed believing in an adversary determined to thwart it. In this light, the everyday human muddle of Immanuel – the differences of opinion, the diversity of temperament – was transformed into something threatening, even demonic. The visions that had once galvanized us began to torment and divide us. At some point, the slow exodus of Immanuelites tipped into a terminal decline.

Many left Immanuel to join other local churches. Others, like myself, gave up on church altogether. Others moved to Lagos, where the miracles and wonders of the Book of Acts were said to be a daily reality. In the years after the peak of the Toronto Blessing, SCOAN had become a popular destination for Immanuelites seeking spiritual adventure or healing. Videos of TB Joshua were passed around. The footage was loud, intense and graphic, full of open sores, tumours and bodily fluids – but who said genuine moves of God would be inoffensive and polite?

'Why do I need to go to Nigeria to see what God is doing, when it should be happening here?' On synagoguevisits.co.uk, Gavin and Susan Winfield's website offering organized trips to SCOAN from the UK, this was one of the Frequently Asked Questions. 'Faith is imparted by seeing and experiencing a present-day move of God,' came the answer. 'The different environment helps expose the depth of disappointment, cynicism and unbelief we live under in the West. It allows the Holy Spirit to renew our minds.'

Breaktime at a Christian healing retreat in rural Hampshire, circa 2002. Several photos show Immanuelites mingling in the grounds of a country house on a sunny afternoon. In one photo, Pastor Graham, seated on a bench, talks to a young Dan Winfield, who looks up to him from the lawn, his knee drawn up to his chin. An overgrown laurel bush looms tall behind them, its leaves dark green and shining. Graham wouldn't live much longer. The cancer, at this point, was already advanced. I'm not sure if the photo is from before or after he went out to SCOAN for healing. The first time, TB Joshua prayed over him and declared him healed. He stopped taking his pain medication as an act of faith. After a few months of declining strength and increasing pain, he went out for prayer a second time.

In the photo, Graham and Dan are arranged in an almost classical pose – the seated elder, the apprentice at his feet. Of course, this wasn't quite right. At the time, Dan was on a short visit home, still in the early phase of his discipleship when it was permitted to maintain relationships from his old life. His mentor was elsewhere.

I left Winchester for Leeds University in 2002, full of anticipation. At university, I thought, I would finally feel at home. I would meet like-minded people. I would find a girlfriend and have Sex Before Marriage. I would get as far away from Christians as I could. It didn't go to plan. I started my second year single, living in a house full of born-again Christians. I blamed my parents, whom I knew had been praying for me.

I'd lived in halls in the first year, and had failed to find friends with whom to share a flat in the second. At the last minute, my coursemate Kirsty came to the rescue: she was in a house with her Christian Union friends and there was a spare room – did I want to move in? I said yes, my relief only matched by my exasperation. It somehow made it worse that they all turned out to be so reasonable and down-to-earth. When praise and worship songs came through my bedroom walls, I'd put headphones on and drown them out with the Dillinger Escape Plan.

At the time I hadn't told any of my Immanuel friends that I was no longer a Christian. That the seemingly unanswerable questions – about hell, suffering, evolution, dinosaurs – had reached a critical mass and overwhelmed the last vestiges of my faith. It wasn't just that I lacked the stomach for confrontation. The conclusions I'd reached felt sad and unedifying; I didn't see much point in spreading the word. Meanwhile, in my house in Leeds, my lack of faith was taken for granted. No-one knew that not long ago, I'd been one of them.

One night, I was walking back from the university library with Kit, one of my housemates. He pointed out a Christian Union outreach event taking place in a large marquee and asked me if I wanted to check it out. Accepting the invitation, I felt the atmosphere between us change. I'd grown to like Kit. He was thoughtful, funny, shamelessly eccentric. He'd sometimes invite friends round to have epic Risk games in the kitchen in full Military-Historical fancy dress. We'd had long discussions about all sorts of things but he'd never proselytized. Now, I was no longer simply his housemate or friend, but a soul to be won. After the event, we left the marquee and headed home. He asked me what I thought of it. I said something non-committal. Then, as we walked past sports bars, kebab shops and groups of drunken freshers, he told me about Jesus.

I don't remember the details of what he said. What stays with me is the strange frisson of doubleness. It was a familiar conversation: the kind of faux-casual chat that we'd drilled at Immanuel as a way of encouraging non-Christian friends along to church. I'd never had the courage to actually have the chat myself. I'd worked up to it, but always bailed, berating myself for failing at this basic Christian duty. The best I'd managed was a stealth evangelism of the most tenuous kind: I'd go to the local record shop, MVC, and deposit CDs by Christian rock bands into the 'Recommended' section at the end of the aisles.

That night, as Kit spoke, I felt a rush of tenderness towards him. I knew how nerve-wracking this kind of thing was. He was a better Christian than I'd ever been. But more than this, I felt elation. It was so sweet to be on

47

the other side. Free from the awkwardness, the guilt, the contorted attempts to reconcile dogma with reason. We walked past the dark expanse of Hyde Park, and life felt like pure possibility.

I didn't let his spiel go on for long. I told him I was a lapsed evangelical. That I knew the words to 'History Maker' off by heart, that I didn't really want to talk about it. He was amused and kind and a little shy, and we talked about other things.

My job as a Psychological Wellbeing Practitioner in the IAPT service lasted three years. Then I moved up the ladder: I got a trainee role as a CBT therapist in the same service. It was shortly after finishing the diploma that my faith in CBT began to waver. This was, perhaps, one legacy of my youth in Immanuel: I'd acquired a real knack for losing faith in stuff.

There was plenty about CBT that appealed to me. I liked its modesty and pragmatism. Wellness did not depend on endless analysis of the psyche and the subconscious. We helped get people unstuck, then let them get on with life. I witnessed, many times, the snowball effect of small changes. I was drawn to CBT's behaviourist roots, and loved the versatility of the functional analysis, which helped you make sense of a behaviour – mental habits like worry or rumination included – by asking what preceded it, and what followed it: both its desired effect and unintended consequences. The elegant perversity of the cycles of depression and anxiety hinted at broader truths. How our ways of escaping fear and hopelessness could give short-term relief while exacerbating the feelings we hoped to escape. How our survival strategies could end up threatening our survival.

My struggles were with the unwritten assumptions

that lay beneath the therapy protocols. In order to gain its status as an evidence-based therapy, CBT had been required to buy into the medical model, a dogma backed by the pharmaceutical industry, whose Bible was the DSM-5, a diagnostic manual which delineated over three hundred disorders. All mental illnesses, according to the DSM, were discrete disease entities, residing in the brain, to be targeted by therapy or pharmaceuticals with the aim of reducing symptoms.

The problem wasn't just the alphabet soup of overlapping disorders, or the fact that some people seemed to be possessed by half a dozen of these entities at the same time. It was the assumption that healthy normality was our default setting, and excesses of suffering were simply deviations to be corrected. That our biggest problem was erroneous thinking, and more rationality was the cure. That our human predicament was something other than tragic, something other than catastrophic. That we were not fundamentally flawed or fallen.

These doubts led me to the third wave of CBT – approaches like Acceptance and Commitment Therapy and Compassion Focused Therapy – which helped mitigate some of its contradictions while retaining and refining its pragmatism. They also got me thinking about Immanuel again.

Doing assessments, I'd lost count of the people I'd spoken to for whom a faith community had been a haven from all kinds of tyrannies: trauma, depression, dysfunctional or abusive families. I'd grown wary of the individualist view of the self that lay behind our training: the psyche as something separate, to be improved and calibrated by its owner. It seemed that people's suffering was often more a result of disconnect – from purpose, from others, from aspects of themselves – than the symptoms of a neatly delineated disorder. There were few forces as tyrannical as an atomized mind turned against itself.

A photo of the Assembly Room of St John's House, soon after we signed the lease for the building in 1993. I remembered those days well. For a few weeks the church diary was dotted with one recurrent event: ST JOHN'S WORKING PARTY. In the photo a group of Immanuelites, armed with spades, are scraping the remains of old carpet tiles from the floor. The old regency-style decor looms behind them: ornate stucco plasterwork on salmon pink walls.

I was in my early thirties when I first saw the photo on the Ex-Immanuelites page. The adults in the Assembly Room, I realized, would have been around the same age back then. Knowing how it all ended was not enough to prevent me from feeling a pang of envy towards them. The older I'd got, the less I'd felt my journey away from church as an uncomplicated liberation.

I'd reasoned my way out of the unhelpful beliefs I'd picked up in my Immanuel youth – the fires of hell, the sinfulness of sex – even if I'd retained a tendency towards shame, and an agnostic theism of the very vaguest kind. But now, seeking reason and liberation from irrational beliefs and arbitrary bonds no longer seemed like an adequate end in itself. My Immanuel years remained a high watermark in my experience of connection. In my secular life, nothing had come close. It was not so much the fire and fervour that I missed, but the putting out of chairs, the laying on of hands, the shared toil towards a common goal. More than the unity of our voices in worship, I missed the warmth in the rough edges: the sound of people falling slightly short of the notes they reached for.

In the photo, sunlight floods the room from the broad windows, hitting the floor in a white blaze. The spade-bearers are arranged around this pool of radiance, each facing a different direction, working their own patch of ground. Their faces are obscured, but they are immediately recognizable from their posture and clothes: James, Gavin, Sean, Anne. The picture catches us in ascent. We are together in this wide open space, turning an empty building into a church.

'Hi Dan and Kate,

Hope all is well with you and the family. I've been putting this off for a while as I realize it may be the last thing you need. But it's something it would be really valuable to have your thoughts on at some point, whenever it's right for you. For a while now I've been wanting to write something – a long-form essay, maybe even something book-length – about Immanuel church and SCOAN...' I sent the email on a Saturday morning, after drafting and redrafting it throughout the week.

I wanted to understand, I wrote, what drew people into SCOAN and kept them there. I wanted to make sense of the links between SCOAN and the revivalist Christianity of our youth. What was it, exactly, that we were all caught up in? I told them of the mixture of longing and dismay that memories of Immanuel evoked in me. At what point did a community turn into a tyranny? Could the belonging that I'd felt in church be separated from that which had led to such division and abuse, such flight from reason?

All this was wrapped up in a tangle of apologies and qualifications. Was it my story to tell? I knew that in some ways it was, but it certainly wasn't my pain. What was merely interesting to me was emotionally wrenching for others in ways I could barely imagine. My drive to pursue these questions was almost matched by the urge to run in the opposite direction.

The following day I got a reply from Kate:

'Hi Matt!

I smiled from ear-to-ear as I read your email out to Dan last night. He was stoking a fire and we got carried away with our own take on Christianity instead of replying you. We have so much to tell you...'

They'd been grappling, she told me, with similar questions. She wrote about the changing nature of their faith. They had recently left the 'mildly charismatic' church they'd been attending since moving to Bristol.

'We saw far too many familiar things which could lead people along similar paths to SCOAN. What "type" of believers we are now remains unclear. Religion can too easily divide and get in the way of friendships, something we don't want to have a part in now. Anyhow! I digress! Let's either chat via a device or over a meal, whatever suits you.'

The next time I was in Bristol was a flying visit. Kate was busy, but I managed to meet Dan on his work lunch-break at a Japanese restaurant in the centre of town. I mentioned that I'd been watching videos of SCOAN disciples being delivered. I asked them if he and Kate had ever got their demons cast out on camera. Dan said that they hadn't. It had only become common practice after they'd left. It was, he thought, a way of getting disciples to discredit themselves on camera, a kind of insurance against future allegations.

The year before they quit SCOAN, a Nigerian ex-disciple called Bisola Johnson, a longstanding member of TB Joshua's inner circle, had released a video called 'Deception of the Age'. In it, she spoke of arranging fake healings for TB Joshua, of being sexually abused by him, and of witnessing his grooming and abuse of the under-age Nigerian girls sent to live in SCOAN as servants of the prophet. Shortly afterwards, Emmanuel TV put out a 30-minute long video about Bisola called 'Beware of Blasphemers'.

Dan explained that after they'd left SCOAN and sent their email, he and Kate had also been dismissed as liars and blasphemers. In conversations, Dan's parents had stuck to the official SCOAN line, saying that every genuine move of God will face demonic opposition. There had been articles online slandering them, Dan said, but SCOAN lacked the material for a Beware of Blasphemers-style attack.

Later, I found the film on YouTube. One section showed Bisola Johnson in a disciple meeting, pleading for forgiveness for some infraction. She prostrated herself on the dirt floor and crawled towards TB Joshua along a row of feet. 'Man of God, help me please,' she cried. 'I have no other place to go. I'm stubborn, I'm proud, I lie... I am the worst sinner here. But I have changed. Please help me. One life in Christ is all I have!' TB Joshua ordered the disciples to pray for her. The camera swept over a line of raised hands. 'The piteous cries for help seem almost genuine,' said the narrator, an American-accented female disciple. 'But having been given a last chance by the Man of God, Bisola's appalling acts and contemptible character only seem to get worse'.

Footage of Bisola's exorcism, from early in her time as a disciple, formed the climax of the film. 'How does the evil spirit affect you?' the deliverer asked her. 'I always behave irrationally,' she said, distraught. 'I don't care about what happens next. Anything my spirit says, I will just do it.' It was not mentioned that moments later, Bisola's evil spirit was purportedly cast out. Her deliverance was first a liberation and then a prison. Now it was a weapon used against her.

The narrator's voice returned: 'What can one expect from such a person?'

Outside a farmhouse to the north of Winchester, around half a dozen cars were parked on a darkened gravel drive. Inside, a group of around twenty people gathered in the dining room to pray. Some shared the visions they felt God had put in their hearts. Others brought Bible verses. Someone had brought a tub of flapjack and passed it around.

The farmhouse, belonging to an ex-Immanuel couple, had once hosted a housegroup, a small sub-unit of Immanuel church which gathered on a weeknight for worship and bible study. That evening, in the months after Dan and Kate's departure from SCOAN, a group of people had come together to pray for the Immanuelites still devoted to TB Joshua.

Madelaine Winfield, Susan's sister, took notes of the first meeting and wrote a summary in an email. Years later, when I met her for coffee, she recalled the atmosphere. It was a strange and sombre kind of reunion. Many of the people who turned up were old Immanuelites. Some had not been in a room with the others since leaving the church. There was a bit of anger, she said, but everyone was united in concern.

The meeting started with a prayer for repentance. Madelaine Winfield spoke briefly, outlining the main points of Dan and Kate's email. People shared their own experiences of SCOAN – many had visited in the past. They spoke of attempts to communicate with the Winfields, discussed potential ways that they could help. Then the prayer and sharing of visions began.

In the years after, the meeting would become a bi-monthly event, with a core of regulars attending. It said something about Immanuel, Madelaine told me, that years after the church disbanded, people would come together to pray like this. I agreed. From Madelaine's notes, I got a sense of the pained humility of the evening. The visions shared did not claim much for themselves, did not prophesy or predict. They were images, instead, of distilled emotion: of hope and helplessness, bewilderment and love. Reading them, I couldn't help but remember the visions once shared in the Assembly Room: the prophecies that had led Immanuel into disaster. Seeking to discern divine truth from the clamour of voices in our heads had not always turned out so well.

Andy spoke of the spirit of witchcraft that reigned over SCOAN. Martha shared a vision of a man in a suit of armour holding his hands over his eyes. Ellen saw an ivory urn that was filled with ashes. The Winfields were standing at a distance from the urn and could not see inside it. She prayed that they would be lifted up to see the ashes inside, and that the urn would be smashed.

II. HISTORY MAKERS

Kate told Sister Celeste that she was going up to the roof to pray. She climbed the staircase of the church building to the top floor, opened the door and walked out into the humid heat of midday Lagos. It was May 2001. The sky was blue and dotted with clouds. The low concrete sprawl of Ikotun-Egbe stretched off into a dusty haze: markets, food stalls, hotels, warehouses. The traffic in Lagos was like nothing she'd experienced back in Johannesburg. Despite the congestion – trucks, oil tankers, battered cars, ancient buses – there was unceasing movement. Cars would beat traffic by bumping over the central reservation and accelerating into the opposite lane. Motorcycle taxis known as *okadas* would mount pavements, dodge pedestrians and weave between trucks.

Kate had heard about the dangers of Lagos: the armed robberies and area boys. When she'd arrived two weeks before, a church minibus had ferried her from the airport straight to the compound, past armed guards and high electronic gates. But the Synagogue Church of All Nations was no haven from the city's relentless pace. The meetings and errands were endless. Disciples ran down corridors clutching paper slips marked with the Prophet's handwriting. Bottle-necks formed outside his office, as dozens of disciples vied for his attention. Every day, hundreds of visitors would arrive, in need of accommodation and prayer. Most nights, Kate didn't get to her dorm room bunk bed until the early hours of the morning, but she still had to wake at dawn. She'd barely had a moment to herself since arriving two weeks before. Standing on the rooftop, breathing in the Lagos air, it felt good to be away from the bustle for a moment. To be alone with God, and to give thanks.

Kate had never dreamed she'd find a place where the presence of God was so palpable, so undeniable. Where miracles straight out of the Book of Acts happened every week: paralyzed people stood and walked; tumours disappeared; people pronounced dead by doctors received prayer from the Prophet and rose again. TB Joshua had already given Kate a nickname – 'Sister Free Spirit' – for the way she would walk with a skip in her step, pick up Yoruba phrases from the Nigerian disciples, and volunteer for the most menial tasks with enthusiasm.

When Kate headed back down the staircase, she saw two disciples waiting at the bottom. One of them told her in a grave voice that Daddy wanted to see her. Walking down the corridor, she wondered what she might have done wrong. She arrived in his office with her usual cheer, unprepared for the fury that met her. 'You want to commit suicide in my church, huh?' TB Joshua shouted. 'You want to bring disgrace on me?'

The office was packed with disciples who had come to witness the scene. Kate was speechless. Sister Celeste had known the rooftop was out of bounds. Rather than warning Kate, she had reported her to the prophet. TB Joshua told her that he would have to send her back to Johannesburg. Kate burst into tears. She wasn't suicidal, she said. She was in good spirits: she was *praying*. The disciples in the office joined the attack. How stupid could she be? What kind of person goes to pray on a *roof*?

Kate had moved to SCOAN in defiance of everyone. Her mum, her aunt, her university friends had all urged her to stay in Johannesburg. Their protests only strengthened her determination.

She hadn't been brought up with religion. Her mum used to tell her how she'd found God without anyone else's help. As a child she'd walk alone to the neighbour-hood church each Sunday morning. In worship and prayer, Kate found a solace and a calm that she could rarely find at home. At school, she joined a group called the Jesus Club, which met for prayer meetings and went on outreach trips to other schools.

Kate always had a difficult relationship with her mum. For most of her life, it was just the two of them around. Kate's dad had left when she was four. She had vague warm memories of his presence, and often wondered why he never visited. Not long after he left, her young-er brother Pete, who had Down Syndrome, was put in a home for children with learning difficulties. He would come home very occasionally on weekends.

Kate's mum had wild mood swings: sinking into deep depressions, flying into violent rages. Certain memories stayed with Kate: mum holding a gun against her own head, threatening to pull the trigger; Kate having to climb out a window to escape her blows. After such outbursts, her mum would say that if Kate told anyone what had happened, she'd kill herself. There were quieter times: her mum found a partner, settled down. They'd have money for a while, live in nice houses. Things would al-ways fall apart before long.

In Kate's mid-teens, her mum married the pastor of a local Pentecostal church. Kate wasn't convinced by her mum's newfound piety. But the pastor seemed like a good man, and she began to attend his church: a lively pen-tecostal congregation. It was here that she first heard of the great things taking place at SCOAN. Her mum and stepdad went on a week-long visit, and came back with stories of miracles, and video tapes of healing which Kate watched with fascination.

After finishing high school, Kate had got a place on a course in Industrial Psychology at Pretoria University. She was excited by the opportunity; as well as the challenge of study, it would be an escape from the drama of home life with mum. A few weeks into her first semester, sitting with her roommate in her dorm, she got a phone call. Hearing her mum's voice, she knew something was wrong. She told her that she didn't have the money to pay her tuition fees. She'd had a solid plan to get it, she said, but there had been a snag. She'd sued Kate's father for years' worth of child maintenance. Her lawyer had insisted she had a strong case, and she planned to pay Kate's fees with the proceeds. When Kate's father found out, he came to Johannesburg, took Kate's brother Pete from the residential home and headed back to his home in Bloemfontein, a city four hours' drive east. He called Kate's mum on the way. You'll see your son again, he said, when you call off the lawsuit.

On the phone, Kate's mum told her not to worry. She said that it would all settle down. Kate couldn't bear to think of Pete in Bloemfontein, dragged away from everyone he knew, held ransom by a man who was a stranger to him. Her brother was suffering because she was studying. Shortly after this, Kate went on the trip to SCOAN. During the visit, her turmoil about her tuition fees began to turn to resolve. Maybe university had been a distraction from her real calling.

Kate's mum and stepdad, though enthusiastic about TB Joshua, did not want her to become a disciple. No-one was more dismayed by her decision than her Aunt Barbara. She'd supported Kate over the years, looking after her when her mum was at her worst, and encouraging her with her studies. She'd been wary about Kate's increasing religiosity, but she'd been delighted at her good grades, and her acceptance at such a prestigious university. After visiting SCOAN, all this seemed so trivial to Kate. She had one purpose in life. To find God and help others do the same.

The rooftop incident was Kate's first glimpse of the dark side of SCOAN. 'That was the start of the breaking down period,' Kate told me. 'I was devastated. I thought I'd found a place where I was wanted and loved. It's only week two and I'm already a disappointment.'

'Every disciple had some version of this experience,' Dan said. 'At any point you'd find out that you're doing something terribly wrong. You'd be called into the office and there'd be all these people accusing you.'

Kate's state of disgrace didn't last for long. TB Joshua forgave her and allowed her to stay. Her relief was immense. 'He pushes you down so low that it feels amazing to be lifted up again,' Kate said. 'You feel grateful: this great Prophet has forgiven me.'

Reporting and punishment was a central part of disciple life. During every weekly disciple meeting, disciples would take turns to report on their brothers and sisters. If TB Joshua deemed a fault to be serious, he would rebuke the disciple loudly in front of the group. The disciple would enter a state of *addaba,* a local word meaning 'correction'. *Addaba* could last a few hours or a few days. The disciple was forbidden to eat, sleep, talk to anyone, enter the dormitory or take a shower. They would hang around outside his office until TB Joshua told them they were forgiven.

Dan and Kate learned to always be on guard. Their fellow disciples would use anything against them: talking about frivolous things; being lazy; being proud. Some disciples made up accusations out of thin air. Reporting, too, was not without its risks: sometimes TB Joshua would side with the accused and turn on the accuser. Disciples would strive for the Prophet's favour all they could, but sooner or later, the *addaba* caught up with them.

This boom-bust cycle served as the engine of disciple life at SCOAN: pushing disciples forward, ever-vigilant, ever-eager to please. Kate and Dan could only see the pattern clearly at a distance, once they had left. At the time, the soaring highs and sudden falls were so intense that they obliterated awareness of anything else.

Over the course of two years, I spent a series of evenings at Dan and Kate's Bristol home. After dinner, they would put the kids to bed, or set them up watching a DVD. Then over white wine or herbal tea, on the tall stools around their kitchenette or around the open fire of their living room, we would have long conversations about their life at SCOAN.

Before I came, I'd imagined interviewing Kate and Dan separately. I'm not sure why – perhaps I thought it would get a more rigorous and forensic account. I was glad I suppressed the impulse. To hear them discuss life at SCOAN was to hear them compare notes, correct each other, mock each other for their former zealotry. They recalled their first impressions of the other – the mix of mutual attraction and annoyance that emerged despite the puritanical strictness of disciple life.

'I used to keep away from you as much as I could,' Kate said to Dan. 'You were always getting in trouble.' But if she'd chosen anyone, she said, it would have been him. One of Dan's very first impressions of SCOAN was of Kate: this attractive South African disciple who'd been really friendly to him on his first visit. 'She was love-bombing me,' he said, smiling. He was referring to the practice of feigning friendliness to attract new members to a cult; they'd both read the anti-cult literature since leaving SCOAN. I suspected, though, that there was nothing calculated about Kate's friendliness.

It was rare for disciples to be anything but single. Many lived a celibate life in dorms for years, even decades. Yet in 2006, TB Joshua told Dan and Kate they should get married. They were asked if they approved, but this was a technicality: saying no would have been a denial of God's will.

I looked at the cork photo board on the kitchen wall: chubby toddlers turning into schoolchildren; nearly a decade's worth of family holidays: up mountains, on beaches. For a marriage mandated by a messianic leader, I thought, they'd done OK. There's a lot you could say about TB Joshua, but he hadn't made a bad match.

On those evenings, there was a lot of laughter. There were gasps of recognition and reminiscence. They had talked about much of this before, but it had been a long time. There were lurches into darkness as Kate spoke about the abuse and the years of suicidal depression that followed.

There were sometimes interruptions. The conversation was getting heavy one evening when Jake, their five year old, pushed the door open and padded into the room in his pyjamas. The silence that fell was a gentle one. He asked if he could show us a dance move that he'd invented. It felt like someone had let sunlight in. Jake was born two years after they'd left SCOAN. He demonstrated his dance with solemn concentration. It was a good move, we all agreed. Kate kissed him and ushered him back to his bedroom. Then we returned to TB Joshua.

'And what about you?' I asked. 'Did you report people?'

'Of course,' said Dan. 'We were good disciples. That was how we rose up the pecking order. But you don't feel like you're breaking down other people. You feel it's bringing you closer to TB Joshua. Which means it's bringing you closer to God.'

'You reported me loads, Dan Winfield,' Kate said. She narrowed her eyes. Dan laughed. 'I tried to make reports that were at least *based* on fact.'

As international disciples, Kate and Dan were spared the corporal punishment inflicted on some of the Nigerian disciples. Kate was three months in when she first witnessed this. She was on office duty.

'TB Joshua had two offices, and a courtyard running between the two,' Kate said. 'He'd told a few of us in one office to stay there and wait for him. Lots of time passed and I started to get bored. Then I heard screaming coming from the other room. And out came this fully-grown man, naked, blood running down his chest. TB Joshua was running after him, shouting. I saw the man's back – this black skin all broken, blood pouring out.'

She later found out he'd been thrashed with a koboko, a leather whip with multiple ends like a cat o' nine tails. A few minutes later, TB Joshua asked to speak to Kate privately. He asked her what she had seen. 'It was almost as if he was blaming me for seeing it,' said Kate.

The man had done something terrible, TB Joshua told her. God had told him this was the only way to change him. It was unfortunate, he said, that she'd seen it. He asked Kate if she thought he'd been wrong. 'I played it down,' Kate said. 'I said: no, no, I'm sure there was a reason.'

I didn't get it. I'd spent two long evenings with Dan and Kate. Each night I'd head back to my brother's house where I was sleeping, my head buzzing with questions I could barely articulate. I couldn't reconcile the people I'd spoken to – free-thinking, irreverent, self-reflective – with the obsessively pious young adults they had once been. How could anyone tolerate the sheer unpleasantness of disciple life? Or be fooled by TB Joshua's manipulations, the crudeness of his teachings?

There had been a certain tone of bafflement in their voices too: the upward turn of Kate's sentences, as if she was faintly surprised at her own words. Dan's constant chiding of his younger self: *so stupid*, he'd say. *So stupid in hindsight.*

I could see how Kate's troubled life in Johannesburg had given her something to escape from; how her childhood may have prepared her to tolerate the emotional turbulence of disciple life. But Dan, like me, had grown up in a family that was close-knit and stable, with all the privileges of a bright middle-class kid in Winchester.

For both of them, it was easy to bring to mind the aspects of SCOAN that eventually made them leave. For Dan in particular, it was far harder to re-inhabit the past self that chose to go there, and chose to stay.

¶ 'I have met with the Holy and Most Exalted God. I have been near to Him and felt His spirit work in my life. Yet I so easily fall away from Him. I have become ashamed of my Saviour and my friend. I enjoy worshipping God. So why do I not feel like it? Why is it a struggle to pray and read the Bible?'

Dan had forgotten he'd ever written these words. We sat in the living room surrounded by piles of papers and lever arch files. It was my third evening at their place. Dan had brought two cardboard boxes down from the loft. He'd told me, cutting through the packing tape, that they hadn't looked at this stuff since they'd left SCOAN.

Rifling through the boxes, he and Kate had found reams of TB Joshua's teachings, notebooks from disciple meetings, to-do lists for organizing foreign crusades, lanyards with their old ID badges attached: their youthful faces gazing back at them with the wide eyes of true believers. Dan hadn't expected to find so many documents from his life before SCOAN.

'I can't remember why I printed these out,' he said, leafing through sheets of diary entries from his late teens. Reading them, I could see why his younger self might have done such a thing. The diaries narrated the first and second acts of a redemption story that reached its climax in SCOAN. Each entry he read had the same mix of drive and frustration: great promise unfulfilled; great gifts squandered.

'I want to be like Patrick, like Hannah, like Catherine, like Sam,' he read, 'but most of all like You.'

'This is sobering,' Dan said, as he leafed through the diary. 'I just wish that someone had given me some really good philosophy books or something.'

Dan grew up in the suburbs of Winchester, the oldest

of four. His father had an executive job in London. His mum, once a nurse, had dedicated herself to children, church and voluntary work. Dan got on well with his siblings. He had a happy childhood. He struggled more as a teenager: he found it difficult to navigate the secular culture of secondary school as a Christian. The Immanuel youth group provided most of his close friendships. Sam Taylor moved in to the Winfields' spare room in 1995. He was Immanuel church's first full-time youth leader. The church leadership had decided that we needed new blood. The first cohort of Immanuel kids were entering their teens, and we lacked youthful Christian role models. Sam was twenty-two when he got the job, the son of a pastor formerly based in Southampton who'd come to Immanuel a few times as a visiting preacher. Sam received a modest salary paid out of tithes, as well as accommodation at the Winfields' place.

'I really looked up to Sam,' said Dan. 'A lot of us did, right?' I nodded. Most Immanuel youth would have agreed that Sam was a bit of a legend. He had cropped brown hair, and wore baggy skater pants and Vans trainers. When he addressed the congregation in the Assembly room, he would pace the stage blocks with a bounce in his step. He was handsome, but not disgustingly so. In the '90s, every boy band had three or four hunks, all smouldering eyes and razor cheekbones, then one who was more or less a normal bloke. Sam was that one.

He had depth as well as charisma. There was a sincerity to him, and an undercurrent of sorrow that lay just beneath his youthful energy. He'd ask us questions that cut through the affected nonchalance of our usual peer-group conversations: What did we want from life? What had God put in our hearts? Even the small talk after Sunday services could be shockingly direct and intimate:

'Hey dude. How's you and God these days?' He listened intently to our answers, as if there was wisdom within us, waiting to be drawn out.

Sam would often tell the story of the path that had brought him to us. He'd had a Christian upbringing, but drifted away from God. He spent his teens chasing the pleasures of the World. After struggling at school, he joined the army, but was medically discharged early in training after snapping his Achilles tendon. In the period of grief and indirection that followed, God spoke to him. He returned to church. He studied at Bible School. Then he came to Immanuel.

He wasn't interested in repackaging the old Christianity. He was a revolutionary. He despaired of the World: its empty consumerism, its nihilistic pleasure-seeking. But he despaired of the Church just as much. So much of what we call church, he used to say, is just dead ritual. The God we worshipped was the same God who brought the flood, parted the Red Sea, raised Lazarus from the dead. But the Church wanted to put Him in a box.

Sam organized interchurch youth gatherings, 24-hour prayer rallies, outreach events, a weekend youth worship session called Catch the Fire. He divided the youth into cell groups that met once a week at somebody's house to pray, read the Bible, and discuss the Christian life.

We learned that there was a secret history of wild Christianity, sidelined by mainstream Christendom: occurrences that spanned continents and centuries in which the faith of normal people had prompted God to manifest in awesome power. The 1904 revival in the Welsh valleys, headed by a young evangelist called Evan Roberts, in which hundreds of thousands of people were converted in dawn-to-midnight big-tent meetings, leaving pub owners without customers, and courts without criminals to prosecute. The Moravian brethren in eighteenth-century Germany, famous for their prayer-watch, in which members would collaborate to pray continuously for years at a time, twenty-four hours a day, seven days a week. The ministry of Watchman Nee in China, whose churches, forced underground by the communist revolution, endured brutal persecution from the government. These movements, we learned, tapped into a vein of divine anointing that was still available to us. Many great men of God had prophesied that greater moves of God were coming soon. If we could cast off the shallow preoccupations of the World and give up *everything* for God, we could be vessels for this same awesome power.

Sam brought a passion for revival to the younger generation of Immanuelites, but it was a passion shared by many others in the church. Dan's parents, who were on the leadership team, were also revival-seekers. They took Dan and his siblings around the world to witness moves of God. They would celebrate the turn of the millennium at Toronto Airport Christian Fellowship, the epicentre of the Toronto Blessing.

It was Sam who encouraged Dan to read more deeply in the literature of revival. Dan read the teachings of Jonathan Edwards, the Protestant theologian who led a revival in eighteenth-century Massachusetts; Smith Wigglesworth, the illiterate plumber from Yorkshire with the gift of healing who became a world-famous preacher in the 1930s and 40s. He read books that spoke to the contemporary state of the church: Tommy Tenney's *The God Chasers*, Rick Joyner's *The Final Quest*.

'The demonic army was so large that it stretched as far as I could see,' wrote Joyner at the start of *The Final Quest*.

'It was separated into divisions, with each carrying a different banner. The foremost divisions marched under the banners of Pride, Self-righteousness, Respectability, Selfish Ambition, Unrighteous Judgement and Jealousy... There were many more of these evil divisions beyond my scope of vision... The leader of this army was the Accuser of the Brethren himself.'

Rick Joyner was not a theologian or a pastor. He lacked any formal biblical training, but had built a worldwide reputation as a kind of radical evangelical seer. He claimed that over the course of a year, while staying in his mountain hut in North Carolina, he'd entered a trance-like state and received a series of visions that he believed were a prophetic message from God. His book, *The Final Quest*, was an account of these visions, which together formed a *Pilgrim's Progress*-style allegorical journey.

'I knew,' wrote Joyner, 'that this army was marching against the church, but it was attacking everyone that it could. It was seeking to pre-empt a coming move of God which was destined to sweep masses of people into the church.'

The most shocking thing about these demonic hordes? They did not ride on horses. They rode on the backs of Christians. These demon-bearing Christians 'were well-dressed, respectable and had the appearance of being refined and educated... [They] professed Christian truths... but they lived their lives in agreement with the powers of darkness.' Moderate, institutionalized Christianity was not just an irrelevance, Joyner suggested. It was not even a mere obstacle to revival. It aided the Enemy in the battle against the True Church. Nothing made Satan happier than a lukewarm Christian.

Sam Taylor started Substance for the Soul in 1997. It

was an annual weekend of study, worship and intensive prayer, held at St John's House, open to any young Christians in Winchester who were passionate about revival. Dan went every year. In 1998, Sam came to the end of his posting as Youth Leader in Immanuel, and became the Pastor of a new church in Barking, East London. In 1999, from this new base, he decided to take Substance for the Soul to a new level. He put together a year-long programme. He would bring together a group of young Christians who were prepared to dedicate a whole year of their lives to God: Bible study, theology, prayer, ministering to local people.

Dan was coming to the end of his A-levels. He'd been accepted for a degree in Development Studies at SOAS in London. He liked the idea of doing some kind of humanitarian work in developing countries, but he had another path ahead of him. At Immanuel, out-of-town preachers would often come to speak at Sunday morning services. In the time of intercession after the teaching, they would pray for people and sometimes prophesy over them. The prophecies were transcribed for posterity; you could ask for print-outs. Over the years, Dan had received a number of such prophecies. He'd collated them in a Word document, a kind of prophetic resumé. They pointed to the same thing: God was going to use him in some dramatic way. He would be instrumental in the coming revival. He deferred his studies and moved to Barking.

In the course of writing this, I came across an old group email from Sam. He sent it a little later, in 2001, when the Immanuelite youth were already scattered. He wished us well, encouraged us in our walk with God. I was at university by then, and long immune to this kind of talk. Revisiting it now, I remembered the appeal it had once held. Sam had been with us at the cusp of our adult lives: a time when we'd been sitting exams, making decisions about studies, jobs, life paths. Amid this pressure to be prudent and forward-thinking, there was something thrilling about Sam's attitude: a mixture of Godliness and kamikaze recklessness.

'Let's press into God,' he wrote, by way of a sign-off. 'Get your eyes off of your life. Keep losing and instead love Him with everything you've got.'

'Maybe the Matrix offers a good explanation,' Dan wrote in his diary, sometime in 2000. 'We are in the Matrix. We have a veil over our eyes. We are controlled by the world system. Once we are saved, we are taken out of the Matrix. We start to see the world through the light of eternity. However, many Christians don't get to this stage. They are only partially awake. They go on being controlled by the world system. Silly boy! How long will it take you to realize that computer games and videos don't help you?'

The Green Room was one of the smaller function rooms of St John's House. It had soft carpet, stackable chairs, a window onto the neat courtyard of the retirement home next door. It was there that Immanuel youth group met for prayer meetings. We also used it for film nights. Sam encouraged us to avoid most secular culture but films – particularly action films – were an exception. We'd rent videos from the Blockbuster next door, order pizza, and wheel in the TV/VCR from the nearby cupboard. As soon as *The Matrix* came out on video, we watched it. It made a deep impression on me too. I loved the slow-motion bullet-dodging and the leather trench coats. I don't remember ever making the connections that Dan made.

During his Substance for the Soul year out, Dan came back to Immanuel for a youth gathering. He gave a talk, and then led the group in prayer. As the meeting went on, he felt a rising anger. People were chatting amongst themselves, making jokes, looking bored. These were his fellow Christians. How could anyone expect God to move when they were so complacent?

In Barking, they'd organized a 24/7 prayer week, praying in shifts throughout the night, asking for God to come into the lives of people in Barking. Along with a number of others, he'd fasted for the entire week. It had been intense. And then it had ended. Not long afterwards, he remembered joining Sam and the others who were watching a film in the living room of their shared house. 'It was a comedy,' Dan told me. 'It wasn't a particularly terrible movie. It was probably a 12 rating.'

He couldn't remember what the joke was – some kind of sexual innuendo. When everyone laughed, he was so overcome with rage that he stormed upstairs to his room. He remembered thinking, 'How is this improving our spiritual life?' It seemed so hypocritical. He remembered the urgency of that prayer week. If they were not using every spare moment to pray, to read the Bible, to push for revival, how could they expect it to come? He was struck that Sam – the person he most admired, who'd pushed him to seek more, to chase God, to reject the World – had been laughing along with the rest of them.

'Oh my God, Dan, you were so annoying,' said Kate. 'Even in Lagos, you were a nightmare.'

When I first emailed Dan and Kate about the book, a choice of two email addresses had popped up as I put Dan's name in the address bar. One, his sensible gmail account. The other, an obsolete address from the early days of email: djdan@ilovejesus.com. I'd forgotten that Dan had had a pair of decks. My older brother Ian did too – they were close friends at the time. In the late '90s they'd play trance music at youth events, complete with dry ice and a lighting rig that someone had persuaded the church to buy. I remembered the four-to-the-floor beats, the swelling strings, the mismatched kick-drum stutter when they fluffed a transition. Rave-style worship was big back then. They'd play music by Christian dance outfits like the World Wide Message Tribe and re:fresh, but also secular acts like Robert Miles and Tiesto. The wordlessness and soaring highs of trance made it a natural fit for worship.

The email address triggered long-dormant feelings in me. Dan was always likeable: reserved but friendly, not outwardly arrogant in any way. He was also the kind of alpha Christian I knew I could never be. He was tall and good-looking. He led prayer with confidence and passion. In worship, he lifted his hands without the self-consciousness that crippled me. I admired and envied him, but as the years went on, I began to smirk inwardly at his Christian sincerity. I don't know if I was present at the meeting where he'd silently raged against his fellow Immanuelites on his visit from Barking. If I was, I'd have definitely been one of the smug chatterers.

When he told the story, though, I remembered harbouring a similar frustration with my church peers. At the time it seemed to me, too, that you had a simple choice: give up everything for God or accept His absence, or at least indifference. The same disillusion that had pushed Dan to study, pray, and seek God with ever-greater intensity, had pushed me away from belief altogether. I never talked to my family or church friends about my doubts. Newly faithless, I found solace in other things. It would be nice to report a descent into sex, drugs and rock and roll. Or an insatiable hunger for literature. In truth, I played a lot of first-person shooters. In *Duke Nukem 3D*, you could pay strippers to show you their boobs, and then turn them into showers of pixelated gore with a rocket launcher. It was so unchristian that it made my heart pound.

Meanwhile, in Barking, Dan was reading John Wesley. In his growing frustration, he'd been possessed by a question. Why did God move so powerfully in some places and not move at all in others? Why did things happen in Pensacola, in Argentina, but not in Barking?

Growing up in Immanuel, we absorbed the sense that a certain amount of doubt and dissatisfaction was part of faith. We learned Paul's words in Corinthians: 'For we know in part, and we prophesy in part, but when that which is perfect is come, then that which is in part shall be done away... For now we see through a glass, darkly; but then face to face: now I know in part; but then shall I know even as also I am known.' To be a Christian was to catch glimpses of God. Only after death would we achieve the clarity that Paul speaks of. In Barking, Dan explored a strand of theology that suggested otherwise. What if we didn't have to wait?

This was what John Wesley, the eighteenth-century Protestant theologian, explores in *A Plain Account of Christian Perfection*. Justification – being converted or born again – was the first stage. At this moment, a gradual process of sanctification begins. A believer gradually renounces sin, and grows in grace. Entire sanctification is the moment in which this process is completed. Most Christians reached entire sanctification shortly before their death: a preparation for coming face-to-face with God. They are so wholly filled with the love of God, so wholly cleansed of sin as to be 'perfect, as our Father in heaven is perfect'. Some, however, are granted entire sanctification earlier in life. There is no reason, said Wesley, why a Christian shouldn't expect this. How could entire sanctification be reached? Only through a tireless pursuit of holiness; a striving to be cleansed from 'all filthiness, both of flesh and spirit'.

'Desire not to live but to praise his name,' said Wesley. 'Let all your thoughts, words and works tend to his glory. Let your soul be filled with so entire a love for Him that you may love nothing but for His sake.'

Dan learned that his striving could still bear fruit. Wesley taught that it was possible to reach a tipping point, a breaking-through. The moment of entire sanctification would be instantaneous, irreversible, impossible to hide: 'The fire would be so hot within him, his desire to declare the loving-kindness of the Lord carrying him away like a torrent.'

Other teachers and theologians picked up the same idea. Different people called it different things. What Wesley called Christian perfection or entire sanctification, others called a baptism in the Holy Spirit. The idea was the same: there is a higher level of anointing, and God wants people to reach it. But this was not a place for the faint of heart.

In *The Final Quest*, Rick Joyner describes coming across the Army of God, a rag-tag band of holy warriors preparing to confront the amassed Forces of Darkness. He then sees a band of Christians trailing the Army of God at a distance. They seem overly happy, as if intoxicated. They play games, feast, sing songs, roam about from one camp to the next. Joyner is reminded of Woodstock. When he tries to warn them of the impending war, they make the peace sign at him. They assure him that God would not let anything bad happen to them.

Towards the end of his year in Barking, Dan had begun to see other Christians in this way – even those that were seemingly passionate and spirit-filled. He'd once been amazed by Toronto Airport Christian Fellowship – its atmosphere of jubilation, its noisy and strange manifestations of the Spirit. It seemed less impressive now. There were too many sensation-seekers and bandwagon-jumpers. The teachings that spoke to him now were the ones that came from a place of raw sorrow and conviction, that spoke of utter submission to God's will, the pursuit of holiness at any cost.

The revival at Brownsville had affected him more deeply than Toronto. There, after the excitement of the early days, the emphasis had turned to penitence and seeking forgiveness for sin. A contemporary report from *Christianity Today* magazine captured it well. 'In some cases, Pastor John Kilpatrick pleads from the pulpit for worshippers to remain calm. "No-one draw attention to yourself," he says. "No-one fracture this holy moment." In other cases, ushers escort the overly exuberant from the sanctuary.'

Dan watched videos of Brownsville at home. The pastor would face the camera and challenge viewers to confess the sins that came between them and God. He felt so convicted of sin that he would fall to his knees, in tears, in front of the TV. Services in Barking also shifted towards penitence. At meetings, young people were encouraged to publicly confess their sins in order to get right with God: envy, unforgiveness, sexual impurity. This sombre turn was in no way a lowering of expectations. It was a preparation for the next wave. It was difficult, awkward, painful work, but God would only pour out his anointing upon the repentant.

The teaching went something like this: We're living in the end times. The Second Coming could happen within our lifetimes. First, a worldwide revival will take place to pave the way for Christ's return. It will culminate in the establishment of an all-powerful world church, led by a new generation of apostles and prophets: a re-establishment of the apostolic church of the New Testament.

The forces of Satan will do anything to oppose the dominion of the Church. And so its establishment will be preceded by a great war. To win this war, a group of elite Christians will be chosen and granted divine powers. They will be known as the Manifest Sons of God. They will heal, prophesy, raise the dead. Some will be invincible on the battlefield. The revivals of the 90s were just the first stirrings of the coming storm. Far greater moves of God – and far greater battles – were imminent.

In the years after leaving SCOAN, Dan read a lot about the history of this narrative. It was this teaching, he said, that left him ripe for SCOAN. You can trace it back through a number of influential Christian movements in the twentieth century: the Latter Rain outpouring that hit a small-town Pentecostal church in Saskatchewan, Canada in the late 40s; the church led by William Branham, a maverick preacher from Kentucky, who was famous for healing and conversing with angels. In the 70s, the Kansas City Prophets took up the baton. Peter Wagner and John Wimber of the Fuller Theological Seminary in California brought it further into the evangelical mainstream, helped along by the Brownsville revival and the Toronto blessing.

Dan pointed me towards a book – *Post-Charismatic* by Rob McAlpine – that critiques this teaching from an evangelical Christian perspective. This helped me make sense of the cultural forces that led Dan to TB Joshua, but it risked taking me further from understanding what it felt like to be him. Summed up in a few lines, the teaching seems nakedly insane. Even at the apex of my own faith, I could not have read it as anything but fantasy.

What revivalist teachers such as Joyner and Tenney articulated most powerfully was dissatisfaction with the status quo. Any restless Christian teenager would find plenty to agree with: church was, for the most part, dull and disappointing. God was not moving in the way we'd hoped he'd move. The place stank of humanity. This was the case, they argued, because we were doing it wrong. After the diagnosis came a vision of the way forward: how to do it right? What would happen if we did?

Just as the dread of a horror movie depends on postponing the appearance of the latex monster, the power of this aspect of the teaching depended on the specifics being vague, glimpsed through a glass, darkly. Perhaps for Dan, some of the appeal of the teaching lay in the act of pursuing it. He was never offered it on a plate. He gleaned it, pieced it together fragment by fragment. He stumbled across connections: between theologians, across eras, between the prophecies of great Men of God and his own prophetic resumé. He borrowed cassette tapes of sermons, read books that led him to other books, had late-night discussions with fellow seekers, watched footage of revival services on VHS.

Tommy Tenney was a round-faced man with round glasses and a goatee beard, the eighth in a line of Baptist preachers. On the video of his sermon at Brownsville, though, there is none of the slick confidence you might expect from this pedigree. He seems like a broken man. He starts by apologising. He's approaching the pulpit, he says, in fear and trepidation. He may not speak as well as other preachers, he says. He may not have the charisma or the flair. But hunger? 'I can outhunger anyone,' he says. He tells the congregation that he's sick of church. An uneasy quiet follows, punctuated by nervous laughter – he sounds like he means it. 'I'm sick of church as Man defines it,' he says. 'I want church as God defines it!'

'I'm gonna say something that might get me banned from this pulpit for life. If Brownsville is the best that God can do...' He pauses. 'If Brownsville is the best that God can do, then we're in trouble...' The YouTube video appears to be uploaded from VHS. It is 1999. The fervour of the mid-90s outpouring at Brownsville has settled down. Tommy Tenney's core message is: 'More Lord. Thanks for what you've already blessed us with. But we want more.'

There are moments in which Tenney is overcome with emotion. It comes like a wave. His voice cracks and breaks and he exhales heavily, as if on the edge of tears. And something wave-like spreads to the wider congregation as Tenney's message builds in intensity. No explanation of the group psychology of such a scene can rob it of its strangeness and wonder. There is a murmuring hum that rises, falls and rises again. A plaintive, unearthly lowing. It is lifted upwards in the slipstream of Tommy Tenney's rising cadences. Some individual voices break through but it is, on the whole, a compound, wordless sound. It is the sound of boundaries dissolving. Of hunger and sorrow beyond language, beyond the self.

I remembered this liminal feeling from Immanuel: how the room could pulsate, how the words of the speaker at the front would be cut off by strange convulsions, as if the membrane between worlds was made permeable and some strange force was leaping across. Where were we, if not on the very edge of something? And if we were on the edge, it stood to reason that we could be on the other side.

Dan went to SCOAN with a group of visitors from the UK. A delegation of disciples greeted them at the airport, led them out into the heat of Lagos, then into an air-conditioned minibus that took them to Ikotun-Egbe. At the SCOAN guesthouse, they drank coffee, chatted, and watched videos of Sunday services on the wall-mounted TV. The scenes on the videos were extraordinary but hard to watch. Women with gaping sores that oozed pus, shown healed days after prayer: healthy skin had grown over the wounds.

Dan soon felt like the odd one out. He was one of a group of eight Brits. Some came with illnesses, seeking healing. Some came out of sheer curiosity, having heard about the miracles and wonders. A few were pastors of evangelical churches. But the ideas that consumed Dan meant little to them. He remembered talking to them about Christian Perfection. They didn't seem to understand.

The disciples at SCOAN were unfailingly friendly. A handful were white South Africans, and the rest were Nigerian. Besides Kate, there was a pair of identical twins – Nigerian women in their early twenties – who took the group on a tour of the complex. They were shown round the church auditorium. At the time it was a huge, open, hangar-like structure, at once humble and awesome in scale: a corrugated iron roof held up with pillars, countless rows of wooden pews over a sandy floor. One of the twins asked Dan about himself. He talked about his year abroad, the frustration of church in the UK, the prophecies he'd had over his life.

Dan didn't tell me much about the first service, but I

can imagine it: the crowds in their kaleidoscopic Sunday clothes, TB Joshua strolling across the stage with patrician ease, Dan in the little huddle of Brits in the VIP section, shuffling to the Afro-pop rhythms of the worship songs. The prayer lines: men and women, old and young, wielding placards – CANCER, DIABETES, AIDS.

What he remembers vividly is the moment halfway through the visit when the twins approached him. TB Joshua wished to see him in his office, they said. They'd been told it was protocol for him to have a one-on-one meeting with each foreign visitor before they left, but this was different – they were only halfway through the visit. He was escorted down a series of corridors, then asked to sit and wait outside the door of TB Joshua's office. Time passed. Then he was called in. As he entered the room, the thick humidity gave way to a sudden coolness. Gentle piano music drifted out of unseen speakers. An aquarium shimmered with goldfish. Screensavers danced on a row of computers. On one wall, a bank of televisions broadcast multiple channels on mute.

TB Joshua sat behind a large desk, smiling his beneficent smile. He asked Dan to take a seat. Dan couldn't believe it was happening. It seemed incredible that he would be singled out like this. TB Joshua asked a question that Dan was entirely ready for, even as it overwhelmed him: 'Do you want to be a prophet?'

'He always knew exactly what to say,' Kate said, laughing. 'If that had been his first line to me, I'd have gone, what are you *talking* about?'

On Kate's first visit to SCOAN, the same twin disciples had shown her around. 'Now it's so obvious that they were his intelligence services,' Dan said. At the time, neither could conceive that from the moment they arrived, they were being eyed as potential recruits. Like Dan, she'd opened up when they'd asked her about herself. She talked about her unhappiness in Johannesburg, her absent father, her volatile mother. She told them that she was smart and hard-working. 'If you need someone like me,' she said, 'I'd love to serve God here.'

On the third day, Kate was reading her Bible in the empty main auditorium when she saw TB Joshua, walking slowly across the front of the church surrounded by a small entourage of disciples. One of the disciples approached her. The Prophet wants to speak to you, he said. She stood up and walked over to him. He spoke in a tone of consolation.

'Don't worry,' he said. 'I will be your father.'

TB Joshua gave Dan money for a flight back. He went home to seek the blessing of his parents and church leaders. Sam Taylor was not enthusiastic. Dan was surprised, given that it was Sam who'd first told him about TB Joshua, and that he'd gone out for a visit to SCOAN himself. Dan was never sure if his reaction came out of possessiveness – Dan had been Sam's protégé in Barking – or discernment.

When Dan met with his parents and Graham, the pastor of Immanuel, he brought the print-out of his prophetic resumé. He showed them how this step was a culmination of years of prophecies. He might stay there for a year or two, he said, then come back to the UK. To his excitement, they agreed. He made his preparations to leave.

At the end of Kate's first conversation with TB Joshua, he told her to come up to his office for a meeting the next morning. She turned up at the appointed time and waited. Finally, TB Joshua invited her in and told her to sit down. He sat in silence for a long time, looking at her. She remained still, confused but loath to break the silence. 'I remember thinking, maybe he's scanning my soul to see whether or not I should stay,' said Kate.

Finally, he spoke. She should go back to South Africa, he said, and think about it. If she felt ready, she should make her preparations to return to SCOAN as a disciple. Whatever had just happened, she had passed the test.

¶ Sifting through the boxes in the living room, Kate picked out a small pile of pocket notebooks. They all had the same simple design: a small wad of lined paper, joined at the top with a single staple, fronted with coloured card and the logo of a Lagos stationers. These were the notebooks she used to make notes from TB Joshua's night teachings. She opened one and looked through it. The night teachings had no fixed time, but it was mostly in the early hours of the morning. The shout would spread through the dorms: MEETING! MEETING! Everyone would get dressed as fast as possible then race through the corridors and down the stairs to the courtyard. Those who arrived first sat on stools. The rest sat on the sandy floor. Any latecomers were sharply scolded for their laziness.

A giant satellite dish stood over them in the moonlit courtyard. Big satellites were necessary in Nigeria, Dan explained, if you wanted to pick up international channels. Whereas in Europe, each individual territory is targeted with a satellite, in Sub-Saharan Africa, a single satellite would fling its signal across a vast stretch of continent, like a great blunderbuss; a normal dish was not big enough to pick up the weak signal clearly.

TB Joshua, sitting on an office chair in the courtyard, would speak the words that God had given to him. They never knew how long the teaching would be, but it would often last hours.

I read a few lines in one of Kate's notebooks. Some were easily legible:

How foolish to neglect the preparation necessary for this inevitable account... TB Joshua is a human just like anyone. The difference is the grace of God inside of me...

Then there are the moments in which Kate loses the battle against sleep. Halfway through a sentence, the words unspool into a single, falling line. Some pages, the battle plays out several times: a push, and then a fall. Another push, another fall.

'You're literally starved of sleep,' Dan said. 'If you're asleep while TB Joshua's awake, you're in big trouble. He didn't have a set schedule but he'd often be awake at 3 a.m. Then you have all these other jobs to do from about half-seven in the morning. You've got to help serve the breakfast for the visitors, memorize notes, prepare teaching. And then you're woken for these night-time meetings.'

I imagined Dan and Kate sitting cross-legged in the sandy courtyard, taking notes, trying desperately to stay awake. This trial was not a punishment but a great privilege. They were participating in history, capturing the divine message of a great Man of God. Most people could never hack it: the exhaustion, the harsh discipline. Dan and Kate could.

I thought of the times in my life when I had, in a brief burst of enthusiasm, joined a gym. The morning after the first workout, I would savour the sweet ache of muscles as I limped around my flat. Far from the pain of injury, this was the intimation of future strength. It never materialized, of course. I kept up the routine for a month or so, then waited another three months to cancel my subscription. In the moment, though, it was glorious: this ache that urged me on towards a new, buff version of myself.

The highs and lows of life at SCOAN were not opposites, I realized. They were made of the same stuff. The difficulties of disciple life only drove Dan and Kate's determination. What was this but the polar opposite of the complacent, hypocritical Christianity that Dan had run away from?

Even the reporting and public shaming of *addaba* was seen as part of their journey towards greater holiness. 'We were taught that persecution was good for the soul,' said Kate, 'even if you got into trouble for something you didn't do.' The more it hurt, the closer it took them to God.

The morning after the teaching, Kate explained, they would do their best to decipher the notes and transcribe them neatly on lined paper. The disciples considered these texts – known as Quotable Quotes – as equal to the Bible in authority. As well as transcribing their own notes, disciples would copy out those of other disciples, often from teaching sessions that preceded their own arrival. They would compile Quotable Quotes into word documents. They would memorize the teachings verbatim, to use in sermons and everyday conversation.

Dan was looking through another lever arch file. He'd found a document in his own neat handwriting. It was a list of statements under various headings: God, the Holy Spirit, Baptism.

'I think this is my attempt at creating a systematic theology of TB Joshua's teaching,' he explained.

TB Joshua was not an educated man. Education, he would say in teaching sessions, was no substitute for anointing. To Dan, TB Joshua's humble background and colloquial Nigerian English made it all the more remarkable that his teaching contained so many finely wrought sentences, so much eloquence and wisdom. Dan was impressed with how consistent it was with ideas he'd studied in previous years.

TB Joshua claimed that his powers came from the fact that he had been baptized in the Holy Spirit: 'It takes someone who is baptized in the spirit to fill people with the spirit. If you are only filled with the spirit, you can't share it. You haven't got it in abundance. Those who are filled should work under those who are baptized.'

He talked about Elijah, the Old Testament prophet of the Northern Kingdom of Israel, known for raising the dead and bringing down God's wrath on idolaters – and his relationship with his protégé Elisha: 'Elisha was not destined to become a prophet but became one through Elijah,' said TB Joshua. 'Elijah was a born prophet. No-one knew where he came from. Born prophets are about one a century. They come without a mentor. Peter and Elisha were not born prophets, but they did greater works.' If the disciples were faithful and hardworking, TB Joshua suggested, they could become his Elisha.

Another idea resonated with John Wesley's idea of Christian perfection: those baptized in the spirit no longer had any will of their own. All their actions were the manifest will of God: 'When you are filled with the spirit you still have your own will,' TB Joshua taught. 'Whereas with baptism you are under the complete dominion of the spirit.'

'Tommy Tenney talked about something like baptism in the Holy Spirit,' Dan said. 'But only TB Joshua said he was able to share it with others. Tommy Tenney just talked about chasing it.'

And yet the teaching was a maze. Parts were bizarre or nonsensical. Certain sections read like fragments of something larger. Pronouns popped up that lacked antecedents. Some bits were plainly unbiblical. Dan vaguely remembered reading strange alternate histories of Moses. He tended to skip over that kind of thing. He'd keep reading, and sooner or later he'd come across something else profound.

This fragmented incoherence, far from undermining

the authority of the teaching, gave it an air of raw authenticity. The reception wasn't perfect, but this was a broadcast from a source greater than TB Joshua. Dan's calling was to untangle it, put it in context, draw out the coherence that was hidden within it.

Dan hoped that serving TB Joshua would eventually lead to his own baptism in the Holy Spirit. 'It was dangled in front of me for years,' he said. 'I was supposed to get there many times. But I kept getting into trouble. And then eventually, after what, three years?'

'Was it 2004?' asked Kate. 'Cape Town was 2004.'

'This was a while before Cape Town. I think it was 2003. TB Joshua told us that four of us foreign disciples – me, Kate, and two others – would be anointed to become Junior Prophets.'

Everyone gathered in the disciple meeting room, the hall that doubled as a dining hall for foreign visitors. They knelt before TB Joshua at the front of the hall. He held out a hand towards them and prayed.

'It was all hyped up,' said Dan 'He'd met us separately and told us we would receive this amazing anointing. He implied that we would receive Baptism of the Holy Spirit. I can't remember if he explicitly said it. But it was what all the teaching pointed towards.'

'I wasn't moved at all,' said Kate. 'I remember actively falling down.'

'Yeah, me too,' said Dan. He sighed. 'If you're going to do a courtesy drop to some random middle-class English person in Southampton, you'll definitely do one for TB Joshua.'

'And you're going to be out for hours!' said Kate. 'I just lay there for ages. I remember thinking, oh gosh, I hope no-one notices that I'm completely conscious here...'

'We could hear him saying, "Now I have prayed for them, and now they are in a trance. God is going to show them a vision." We weren't told what to say before. You had to come up with something. But it's not a conscious thing, like "I'm faking it."'

'I knew I was at that point,' said Kate.

'No, but at the time it's more like – I really need to listen to this...'

'Right,' said Kate. 'It's like, please God, please God, give me something...'

'Exactly, yeah,' said Dan. 'I can't even remember what I said. But it was fairly easy. I had prior training – it was like the pictures we used to have in Immanuel. Something vaguely spiritual.'

'Yeah, anything,' said Kate. 'I can't remember mine either. Maybe some trees or something.'

After they got up, newly anointed, they didn't feel any different. But their lives changed. Their position at the top of the hierarchy of disciples was assured. For the most part, this meant that they were even busier.

'It was flipping annoying actually,' said Kate. 'When some old lady arrived at the gates at 4 a.m. asking for healing, you'd be woken with a phone call. "We need a junior prophet!"'

They'd spend hours and hours each Sunday praying for the people who'd come for healing from TB Joshua but didn't make it to the main prayer line. 'It was almost like a top-up,' said Dan. 'They were told "keep coming back, and they'll keep praying for you and you'll get a little better, because these junior prophets have a little bit of TB Joshua's anointing."'

It was 2005. TB Joshua was visiting the SCOAN branch in Ghana for a crusade. There was a crowd of tens of thousands, filling the church and overspilling to the grounds outside. There were giant TV screens at the front of the church, and a camera crew that followed TB Joshua around.

The service had been going on for hours, and they'd reached the climactic healing section. TB Joshua was walking down the prayer line laying hands on people, accompanied by Dan and other disciples. Then a group of men approached.

'Prophet, prophet, there is a lady outside,' one of them said. 'She's lying down. She can't walk!'

TB Joshua followed them, his entourage and camera crew in tow. Outside was a huge unlit parking lot with a dirt floor. Crowds of people were gathered in the darkness to observe an elderly woman in traditional Ghanaian dress, lying on a mattress under the halogen lights of the camera crew.

Dan wasn't forewarned. He assumed that TB Joshua would pray for her. Instead the prophet turned to Dan: 'OK, go and lay down on her.'

Dan knew that the instruction had biblical precedent. Elisha, the great prophet and protégé of Elijah, had raised a young boy from the dead in this way. *He got on the bed and lay on the boy, mouth to mouth, eyes to eyes, hands to hands.* At the same time, he didn't want to lay on top of an elderly woman in a car park, on live TV.

'You don't have much time to think things through,' Dan told me. 'It's a huge pressure. You've got this big angry man. Well, not angry, but...'

'Well, he *is* angry,' said Kate.

'He's incredibly intense. So you can't just say, "Um, can I clarify what you meant by that?"'

At the time, TB Joshua had forbidden Dan from cutting his hair. His long, dark blonde hair was combed back and stiff with gel. He kneeled down beside her at first, raising his hand in prayer. TB Joshua immediately shouted at him: 'No! Lay on her!'

Next, he leaned over her, trying to be vaguely obedient while avoiding actual bodily contact, but TB Joshua was still unhappy. 'I think he might have even pushed me down,' said Dan. Finally he lay on top of her with all his weight. Hands to hands and eyes to eyes, if not mouth to mouth. 'Thank God this happened before YouTube existed,' said Dan.

One of TB Joshua's helpers held out a microphone to Dan as he shouted as loud as he could: 'In the mighty name of Jesus Christ, be healed, be healed, be healed!'

The foreign disciples often got the high-profile jobs, but the inner circle of Yoruba-speaking Nigerians kept the show on the road: editing prophecies, finding candidates for healing and exorcism, sorting the hopeless and un-photogenic from the TV-friendly cases. A group of female disciples known as the Emergency Sisters did many of the key tasks. This division of labour allowed some of the manipulation to remain invisible to at least some of the international disciples. International disciples saw no end of signs and wonders. For the most part, they missed the smoke and mirrors that lay behind the miracles. When they did witness suspicious things, the pressures and perils of disciple life dissuaded them from dwelling on the deceit.

Kate had arrived in the car park half an hour before Dan. She'd been told to help clear a space for the healing. She came across an elderly woman standing in the middle of the allotted area. She told her to move. The woman walked over to one side. Suddenly, one of the Emergency Sisters came up to her from behind, shouting: What are you doing? She pushed Kate aside and moved the woman back to her original position. Soon afterwards, the elderly woman lay down on the mattress in time for TB Joshua's arrival. Kate was horrified: she'd been pushing around the star of the show. The main thing on her mind was not the fakeness of the healing, but the possibility of *addaba:* would she be reported for nearly messing the whole thing up?

Dan, lying on top of the Ghanaian woman under the gaze of the crowd and the camera crew, didn't know any of this. He just knew that this was a big deal. It could be the culmination of all his prayer and striving, a fulfilment of years of prophecies. Or it could be his biggest failure.

He tried to summon up his faith. 'I'm Elisha,' he thought. 'I'm just like Elisha.' But his mind raced with doubts. Had he been there too long? Was it getting weird? What if he got up too soon, and she wasn't healed? Eventually, TB Joshua tapped him on the back. 'It's enough,' he said. 'Tell her to get up and walk.'

Dan stood up, his heart pounding. The crowd was hushed. The helper held the microphone up to him. 'Get up and walk,' he said.

The woman got up from her mattress and walked.

III. THE GIFTS OF THE SPIRIT

THE LETTERS

After dictating a letter, the Apostle Paul would some-times take hold of the pen. 'I, Paul, write this greeting in my own hand, which is the distinguishing mark in all my letters,' he wrote to the church in Thessalonica. 'This is how I write. The grace of our Lord Jesus Christ be with you all.'

In some letters, he would finish with news about his travel plans. 'I shall come to Corinth after passing through Macedonia,' he wrote to the Corinthians, 'and I may stay with you, perhaps even for the whole winter.' Sometimes he would ask favours, as in his letter to Timothy, purport-edly from a prison in Rome. 'When you come, bring the cloak I left with Carpus at Troas, and the books, above all my notebooks...'

Nothing ruins the Bible like being a teenage evangelical. When I was a child, I understood as a child, absorb-ing Bible stories in all their strangeness, untroubled by any need to arrive at clarity or truth. Later, in my teens, there was more at stake. To not read the Bible was to be a terrible Christian. But the thing was a minefield. I'd sometimes open it at random, praying to land on a pas-sage that felt like a message from God. Every time I found something that provoked doubt – a genocide, a brutal or bizarre edict – I would shut the book quickly and do something else. It seemed safer to just feel guilty for not having read it.

Did I ever read Paul's epistles back then? Many pas-sages were familiar. But it was only now that I appreciated the vividness of these letters: not just the teaching, its paradoxes and startling imagery, but the glimpses into everyday life. The names of patrons and protégés, the intimate bonds and bitter rifts. The hopes and fears, the plans gone awry. They were reminders that the text was once a scroll, was once delivered by a messenger, who travelled by boat across the Mediterranean or on foot along Roman roads. That in some first-century room, a group of people had once gathered to hear it read aloud for the first time. The second-person form of the letters collapsed time and distance. The words of fraternal love still held a human warmth. The admonishments ('you stupid Galatians!') retained their spittle-flecked wrath.

What did we believe in Immanuel? We believed in the Father, Son and Holy Spirit. We believed in the truth of the Bible. We rejected the inherited baggage of denominationalism, and looked straight to scripture for a model of how to do church.

We believed in the gifts of the spirit, granted to believers to sustain and strengthen the church. Paul spoke of these in his first letter to the Corinthians. Some gifts of the spirit seemed more supernatural, strange to outsiders: the gift of tongues, prophecy, and healing. Others were more mundane: the gift of teaching and administration. All the gifts had their place. They did not exist for the glory of the individual, but for the edification of the group.

Edification. The moment I came across this word, re-reading Corinthians, I saw the frowning figure of my dad, looming in the doorway of my teenage bedroom. 'Is this really edifying?' he used to ask, in response to the computer game I was playing, or the shouty music I was listening to (the fact that it was *Christian* heavy metal did not wash with him). I didn't need to know the definition of the word; it was all in the tone, which also told me that

96

he already knew the answer.

Maybe this was partly why I found the character of Paul so compelling, re-reading him now. Why I could go from loving him to hating him in the space of a sentence. There was a lot of Paul in my dad's parenting style: his warmth and attentiveness, his infuriatingly rigid sense of Good and Evil that seemed impossible to challenge. These days, after an evening binging on computer games, or immersed in the stupider corners of the internet, this voice would often turn up in my head. *Is this really edifying?* It turned up a lot as I tried to write this chapter, revisiting Immanuel and its disastrous end.

Was this edifying? Was I building up or pulling down? The doubt was mostly mine. I'd interviewed my parents for the chapter, and they expressed no such misgivings. I'd been surprised, when I'd asked some old Immanuelites to talk, how eager they were to share their thoughts. Most remained practising Christians, but we had common ground. Immanuel was a profound experience for all of us. We agreed it was a community that had got something right, though the nature of this *something* was harder to define. And we agreed that it had gone horribly wrong.

It was too late, in any case, to edify or attack. Immanuel was gone. I was uninterested in returning to the evangelical fold, and equally uninterested in undermining the faith of those who'd remained. But I had a mystery to pursue. Was the revivalism that took Dan and others out to SCOAN a kind of contagion, a mutant strain of Christianity that had crossed the Atlantic like an airborne virus? Or was it a tendency that was latent in the church all along? Could I untangle what I missed about Immanuel from that which had led to such hubris and division?

THE GIFT OF TONGUES

The nicest thing about playing the bass in the worship team of Immanuel was the bass itself. It was a Fender Precision, American-made, with an Amber Sunburst finish. I loved its heft, the hardwood glide of the neck, the taut metal thrum of the strings.

It had been gathering dust in the PA cupboard since the old bassist left. I was around 14 when the worship leader asked me to join the band. I quickly said yes. I'd never played the electric bass, but I'd had a few double bass lessons at school. I kept the volume low for the first few months, as I was hitting as many wrong notes as right ones. I wore the bass low-slung at first, and it made me feel cool in a way that I hadn't felt before, though it was far too big for me, and I eventually took to sitting down on the amplifier so I could reach the lower frets.

I was grateful to be asked to join, but I was faintly embarrassed by the band. At home I listened to Christian rock music, and secular Britpop taped off the radio. There were other churches – like the Community Church down the road in Southampton – that had far better bands, with Stratocasters and fuzz boxes and fat Marshall amps. In Immanuel the line-up varied every week, but the sound was always tame and anaemic. There was a keyboard player, an acoustic guitarist or two, a drummer if we were lucky, and a clarinet player whose sprightly embellishments were the polar opposite of rock and roll.

On some Sundays, however, we made a sound in Immanuel that was unlike anything I've heard since. It didn't happen every week, and only ever lasted a couple of minutes at most. It was always at the end of one of the slower songs – 'Be Still', or 'What a Friend I've Found', or 'My Jesus My Saviour'. After the last chorus, the worship leader would signal for the band to play on. We would circle around the refrain, our tone hushed, our tempo slightly slowed. And then the congregation would begin to sing in tongues.

How to describe it? A few dozen people opened their mouths and something – not English, not any human language – came out. Each person sang their own tune around the simple chords, formed of their own strange non-words. There were moments when it was all chaos and dissonance, a primordial soup of sound. Other moments, the voices coalesced into crystalline harmonies, then fell away again, only to find their way into some new fleeting form. The voices became a kind of murmuration, a spectral body in constant flux.

People believed that when they sang in tongues, the Holy Spirit sang through them. I never had the strength of belief or confidence to speak or sing in tongues myself. In the last days of my bass-playing in Immanuel, I'd look out to the sea of lifted hands and be hit with a feeling of desolation. That they might be singing to a big nothing seemed almost unbearably sad to me. But somehow the radiance of that sound survived my disenchantment.

Out of all the gifts of the Holy Spirit, few have caused more disagreement among Christians than the gift of tongues. For many early US Pentecostals, the gift meant an instant fluency in foreign languages, divinely bestowed for the purposes of missionary work. Alfred Garr, an evangelist linked to the 1906 Asuza Street revival in Los Angeles, believed that he spoke fluent Bengali until the day he arrived in Calcutta.

In Immanuel, many believed that tongues contained divine messages. After someone came up to the microphone to speak in tongues, another person would come to share a tentative interpretation – usually words of encouragement, rarely anything too concrete. When Immanuelites sang in tongues together, though, it was not the content of speech that mattered. To sing in tongues was to be untethered from language, to become pure song.

How can I fathom my attachment to this sound? Watching YouTube videos of big-shot American preachers speaking in tongues at the pulpit, I feel sickened by the smug showmanship of it. Anyone can babble like this. All you need is disinhibition, a state that might be brought on by profound spiritual experience, but which is easily accessible to those who are shameless in the first place. Here, the charisma sells the product, like the mail order qualifications on a quack doctor's wall.

Yet the sound I recall from Immanuel – that shifting mass of voices, at once singular and plural – was a very different thing. Perhaps it was not the sound itself but the possibilities of togetherness contained within it: this momentary communion which was egoless, leaderless, utterly sincere.

Dan's story of becoming a disciple at SCOAN had fascinated me because he'd followed to its farthest reaches a path that we'd once walked together; one that I'd only ever wandered partway down. My own teenage God-chasing had been inept, undramatic, never more than half-arsed. Yet Dan's relentless striving towards breakthrough, his oscillation between self-belief and brutal self-reproach, felt intimately familiar to me.

This was undoubtedly part of Immanuel's legacy. It was there that we learned – through the likes of Tommy Tenney and Rick Joyner – to see ourselves as the lone heroes of our own epic dramas, capable of achieving awesome things if we could only stop doubting, cast off the complacencies of tradition and pray really, really hard. We learned that we were history makers, and if we didn't see dead men rise or the blind set free, it was because we simply weren't passionate enough.

This revivalist Christianity often sold itself as an antidote to the empty pleasures of Western consumer society. What strikes me now is the extent to which it mirrored, in its endless drive for growth and sensation, the culture it claimed to oppose. I had little nostalgia for this aspect of Immanuel, but then I never really left the restlessness behind. It just changed focus, latched onto other things.

There was another side to Immanuel. Not the lonely striving of revivalism nor its mass elation, but a kind of collectivity that seemed antithetical to these things. A feeling of holding and of being held. A sense of fellowship and interdependence whose absence I felt keenly in my secular life.

My very first memories of Immanuel were of dust. In our rented meeting room in Winchester Guildhall, the morning sun would descend in diagonal shafts from a row of skylights in the ceiling. When one of these columns touched down near my seat, I would watch it closely. From a distance it seemed as solid and sharp-edged as masonry. Up close, it was an edifice made of movement: all eddy and flow, streams emerging and unravelling. As I watched, sitting with my family, the sounds of Immanuel would unfold around me. The polyphony of familiar voices, the words now earthbound and banal, now sacred and soaring. The pulse of electric piano and shimmer of acoustic guitar. The warm and ragged song of the congregation; the words I knew by heart before I knew their meaning.

I'd sometimes track a single particle of dust as it

traversed the pillar of light. Occasionally it would flash minutely as it caught the fullness of the sun's rays. When it reached the outer edge of the pillar, it would pass quietly back into invisibility again. It occurred to me, at some point, that the shafts of light had something to do with the things that the adults spoke about: God, love, the Holy Spirit. There was no urgency to know for sure. Nothing was required of me but to sit there, held in the radiance of the voices and the songs.

By the time I was in my early teens, this state of absorption had given way to something more fraught. Often, sitting alongside my peers in the Assembly Room of St John's, I was aware of little but the gap between what I should have been feeling and what I felt; what I should have been thinking and the thoughts that turned up. I knew that I was called upon to praise, but could rarely bring myself to do it, could not understand why an omnipotent creator would demand such displays; could not raise my hands without feeling a kind of stage fright, a sense that my insincerity would show, that everyone would see that I wasn't doing it right. I was tormented by new hungers. Certain Sundays – the weather warm, the room bathed in sunlight – it would occur to me, with the force of a Damascene vision, that there were knickers under every Sunday dress. I'd imagine the delicate cotton, the unfathomable wonders beneath, and as everyone rose to sing I'd stay seated, an elbow resting on a raised knee, my eyes closed as if in prayer. The more I pushed away the sinful thoughts the more relentlessly they intruded. The more I strove to feel the presence of God, the further away He seemed.

And then I joined the worship team. At first, the sheer focus required to hit the right notes made any doubts or bad thoughts impossible. Even after my growing confidence allowed for a wandering mind, I was less vexed. The thoughts didn't go away, but I felt suspended above them, held in the equanimity of being of use. All that really mattered was that I played the bass.

It wasn't an exciting role. It was almost boring, but without boredom's agitation. There was a rightness in the restraint it demanded. My notes, dull and inadequate on their own, joined with the sound of the band, underpinned the melodies. Together, we built a structure that held the voices of Immanuel and allowed them to ascend.

After I left Immanuel, the word corporate never had a positive connotation. In my late teens I'd dismiss certain bands for being too corporate, with the righteous zeal of an indie kid. A leftist student in the No Logo era, I'd learn about the insatiable appetites of multinational corporations, about the concept of corporate personhood, the concept by which companies in the US could claim the legal rights of an individual. Yet the word always retained a shade of its first meaning. In Immanuel, our pastor Graham would often speak of the church as a body, about the value of corporate worship. I don't recall ever hearing an explanation of this term. I absorbed its meaning in other ways.

The idea of church as body goes back to Paul. 'We were all brought into one body by baptism,' he wrote in his letter to the Corinthians, 'whether we are Jews or Greeks, whether slaves or free men... There should be no division in the body, but that its parts should have equal concern for each other. If one part suffers, every part suffers with it; if one part is honoured, every part rejoices with it.'

In *Darwin's Cathedral*, the evolutionary biologist David Sloan Wilson took this metaphor seriously as a hypothesis to be tested. He explored the ways in which a religious community might work as a kind of superorganism. He showed how a doctrine – like the one laid out in Paul's letters to the early churches – can work as a blueprint for the functioning of a group. The doctrines that persisted were the ones that helped form groups that thrived, expanded, and reproduced. Seen this way, the truth value of a doctrine was less important than the fruit that it bore: the relationships that formed around it; the things it made happen in the world.

This idea was exciting and unsettling to me. The way it looked beyond the binary of true/untrue. The way it allowed rigour and scepticism to co-exist with a certain awe and reverence: that of a scientist marvelling at an organism's endless, elaborate ways of defying entropy.

Darwin's Cathedral helped me pinpoint what captivated me about Paul's letters. To read them was to eavesdrop on this extraordinary point in history: the moment in which a small radical Jewish sect in the Middle East – one among many – turned outwards to the gentile world and transformed into something that would span continents, spawn countless mutations, provide a shape and structure for countless lives.

Sloan Wilson's talk of superorganisms also spoke to me more intimately. It captured something I'd known from Immanuel but had struggled to name. Preparing to write the first chapter of this book, I spent hours reading through the archive of church magazines I'd borrowed from a friend. I wanted to trace the point at which the mania for revival had seized us. My plan was to go through the decade's worth of issues systematically, marking the mentions of revival with post-it notes as I went. It shouldn't have taken long, but I kept getting waylaid. To read the magazines was to hear the living voice of

Immanuel again, in all its variousness:

A minibus going FREE to anyone who will take it away. It goes, but it needs attention! See Pete or Helen if interested.

A massive thank you from the Hartridges, to those who put us up (or put up with us) over the last few months. There aren't many people who could take on two people, a baby and a dog. We don't where God is leading us with the business, but we know that we are in the right place at the moment.

A list of things to do during a boring sermon:
1. See how many words you can make out of 'Methuscla'.
2. Locate all the typing misteaks in the church magazine.
3. Slap your neighbour. See if he or she turns the other cheek. If not, raise your hand and tell the pastor.

'A Night in the Life of a Church Treasurer'
The church finances are my hobby. Some people build models, some tap dance, I put little figures in lines in books. What I do would send most of the sane population completely round the bend. It's probably just as well that I'm left to myself for most of the time. To start in my usual positive style, let's begin with the things I really do not like...

There were intense but civil debates – on creationism vs. evolution, on organic farming vs. agribusiness – that ran across issues. There were kids' stories: Gavin Winfield's sci-fi parables; my dad's Teenage Mutant Hero Angels. There were life stories – accounts of growing up in South Africa, of following God's call to re-train as an accountant, of surviving childhood sexual abuse, of emerging from suicidal depression. Their endings were cautiously redemptive: 'Since then, the going has been far from easy.

But I'm certain now that God does have a plan for my life. Psalm 91 is a constant stronghold for me: He will cover you with his wings. You will be safe in His care; His faithfulness will protect and defend you.'

I found myself drawn, without knowing why, to the dullest parts of the magazines: the diaries, the rotas, the tables. In the diary section, the addresses of the houses where we met for cell groups, Bible studies and social gatherings. The list of names on the Stewarding Team rota, which each Sunday assigned a group to arrive early to prepare the hall then stay late to put everything back.

These were the remains, I realized, of the once-living organism that was Immanuel. For all their dryness, they evoked the life that once pulsed around them. In one issue, the diary had a notice for a 'Kids' Club Tramps Supper', when us kids would spend the evening walking a winding line through the city from one Immanuelite home to another, being fed – homemade pizza, rice crispy cakes, Monster Munch – at every stop. Several issues had reports of baptisms. I remembered, looking at the grainy black and white photos, how we would finish the Sunday service early, put on our coats and make our way through the city as one, stretching single file along the narrow pavement of Eastgate Street, then gathering around the riverbank to witness a church member being born again.

The rituals and repetitions, the rightness on the edge of boredom, the rare moments of transcendence – these were all aspects of the same feeling. Not just that of connecting with others, but of being more than one. It was nice to be a superorganism.

In my post-Immanuel life, my yearning for togetherness has been matched by a need to be alone and unencumbered that borders on misanthropy. But I've had brief snatches of a similar feeling. Getting the vote out at election time: the doorstepping in the rain, the end-of-day meet-up in the pub, the unfamiliar optimism that lasts as long as the badge stays on. At Moving Voices, the friendliest Open Mic night in Southampton, listening to a first-timer earnestly butcher a tune: the pained, reverent hush; the respect for the principle of song that trumps the shittiness of the actual song. And playing in bands, too. It's probably no coincidence that some of my most enduring friendships are with old bandmates: those with whom I've hauled equipment, argued about arrangements, practised songs to death, shared delusions and occasional epiphanies.

Once I noticed the superorganisms in the church magazines, they started turning up elsewhere. Reading through the transcripts of my conversations with ex-Immanuelites, I'd catch sight of their outlines in the stories people told. There were the car-pools, the working parties, the financial gifts for those in need. There was the mum who, for several weeks, breastfed the newborn of another Immanuelite woman while she was hospitalized with viral pneumonia and forced to isolate from her baby.

There are good reasons to be wary of this intense form of collectivity. There were conspicuous limits to compassion; my petty teenage torments would not compare to those of an Immanuelite growing up gay. We wouldn't get misty-eyed about togetherness if it was the Borg or the Ku Klux Klan, but the stories I heard were of a collective that had some room, at least, for the untidiness and idiosyncrasy of the self. I asked Teresa, the former church treasurer, what she most missed about Immanuel. She'd joined aged nineteen, and had collected tithes and managed the finances for almost two decades as a volunteer.

'I remember once I was going through a really bad spell,' she said. 'I'd been walking around Winchester all night, in desperation, thinking, "I don't know how to do this anymore." I ended up at the Smiths' house. They didn't know I was coming. I just waited for the lights to go on in the house then knocked on the door. Lynn was sort of like "Oh, hello. Are you coming for breakfast? I've got my parents here, and my cousins, but come join us!" These were the sort of relationships that came out of Immanuel. It was alright to be in a mess but still be part of it.'

There was something quietly counter-cultural about a group that made possible this kind of mutual sustenance and selflessness, this kin-making beyond the confines of the nuclear family. It was this everyday side of church that revivalists most disdained. 'God is tired,' wrote Tommy Tenney in *God Chasers*, 'of being second place to everything else in our lives. He is even tired of being second place to the local church program and church life!' What were the rotas, the coffee mornings, the mundane routines of stewardship and service, but proof of lukewarmness?

Tenney mocked complacent churches as 'bless me clubs', imploring God to 'ruin anything that isn't You!' He came across a bit like Elijah, if he'd spared the prophets of Baal and called down God's wrath on a church picnic instead. This was not born of malice, but sorrow at God's distance, and a belief that He could give us more.

Tenney spoke of humility, brokenness, the dismantling of the ego. In the same book he also spoke of a God who could turn each individual seeker, freed from the fetters of humdrum community life, into a superhuman. 'How long has it been since your shadow healed anyone?' he wrote, invoking the purported miracles of the evangelists

Charles Finney and Smith Wigglesworth. 'How long has it been since your mere presence in the room caused people to say 'I've got to get right with God?' It was this hunger for disruption and horror of stasis that took hold of Immanuel.

Perhaps I loved the sound of singing in tongues for its rarity. It couldn't be replicated or faked. It could never have existed without the singers believing they were channelling something divine and eternal. When, playing bass in the band, I first started doubting its divinity, the sound became tragic and farcical. Recalling it as an adult, the question of its provenance mattered less. The beauty lay in its transience, its very human finitude. We raised our voices. Strange and wonderful forms emerged then fell away.

I remembered, at the very end of the meeting, the odd tenderness of the in-between time: the minute or so after we put down our instruments and before the hall emptied out. Some people remained in small prayer huddles. Others would start gathering up their coats. People on the floor would begin to sit up, blowing their noses, dabbing eyes, adjusting rumpled clothes. There were little exchanges that bridged the gap between sacred and mundane speech: a 'God is good' and a hug; a squeezed shoulder and a hallelujah like a sigh. As I switched off the amp, coiled the jack lead and placed the bass in the velvet bed of its flight case, I'd see people heading for tea and conversation in the dining room next door. Then the stewarding team would wheel in the chair-trolleys and start stacking, turning the church back into a hall.

THE GIFT OF PROPHECY

'He who prophesies,' wrote Paul in his letter to the Corinthians, 'speaks to men for their edification, encouragement, and comfort.'

In every issue of the Immanuel church magazine, the prophecies shared on Sunday mornings were transcribed in full. In the earlier issues, the prophecies were often words of comfort rather than predictions. 'You are My jewels, each one of you,' read one of them. 'However small, however insignificant you feel, you're a jewel in My crown. I love you so much, My children.'

As time went on, the visions seemed to get grander, more martial, more confident of what the future held. The church as rocket, primed for take-off, as tank heading into the devil's territory. Then, some time in the mid-1990s, the passive-aggressive prophecies began.

Someone had a vision of a gushing geyser amid a barren wasteland, its water raining down on the people of God. The people were enjoying the water, dancing in the shower, allowing it to bring healing and cleansing to their bodies. But some people were saying that the water was too hot and too intense. They started to put up umbrellas to keep off the rain.

Someone had a vision of a wellspring. The Lord said that inside each one of us there was a wellspring of living water which we could draw from every day. But some of us, said the Lord, were not drawing from it. We might not notice this, He said, when we were walking through green valleys filled with dew, or walking with others whose well we could draw from. Some of us, He said, were very good at drinking from other people's wells. But the Lord said that if we didn't learn to drink from the well that he'd placed within us, then what would we do when the going got tough?

When the London Brothers could no longer fit in a living room, they moved the meeting to the Leprosy Mission Hall. When the owners complained that their dancing endangered the structure of the building, they moved again. By the time they started meeting at the London School of Economics, several hundred people were attending.

This wasn't church, exactly. It started at the tail end of the 1960s as a brotherhood of leaders, a regular gathering of young men who led new churches around the UK. Each of their churches had started as small, informal meetings and had expanded. They'd all broken away from traditional congregations – Brethren, Salvation Army, Calvinist, Anglican – in search of something more vital, unconstrained by legalism and dull liturgy. 'We were green as green could be,' said Gerald Coates, recalling the beginnings of what would become a house church in Cobham, Surrey. 'We thought we were the only people in the world who loved Jesus and didn't go to church on Sunday.'

The first gatherings of the London Brothers marked the moment when these leaders discovered they were part of something bigger. The convictions that had left them estranged from their old congregations were shared by others with an equal intensity. They were not merely oddballs or splitters but the vanguard of something radical and unknown. By the early 70s, the initial core of house church leaders was far outnumbered by men and women who'd got word of the ecstatic atmosphere of the gatherings.

The meetings had no structure, no leadership. What bound the attendees was a rejection of human traditions and hierarchies, and a belief in the gifts of the spirit. If people simply turned up in faith, they believed, the spirit would turn up too. The wager seemed to work. There was free-form worship, wild dancing, the laying on of hands. There were spontaneous readings of scripture, words of knowledge and prophecy. In this collective casting-off of bonds, intense new relationships were formed.

What kind of church was Immanuel? I never knew how to answer the question precisely. Some people called us a house church, though we only met in houses for the first few years. Evangelical was another familiar term, though Immanuel differed from the American megachurches commonly associated with the word. I remember being told that we were just Christians. Not Anglican, not Catholic, not Baptist: just followers of Christ.

It wasn't until writing this book that I learned there was a name for us. We were restorationists. The meetings of the London Brothers, vividly described in Andrew Walker's book *Restoring the Kingdom*, were the crucible out of which this movement emerged. The lineage was clear. Immanuel was started in the early 1980s as a church plant by members of Southampton Community Church, whose leader, Tony Morton, was an early restorationist.

I recognized so much of Immanuel in Walker's account of the genesis of restorationism. That feeling of collective self-creation, at once joyful and deeply serious, at once irreverent and fundamentalist. The anecdotes in the book mingled in my mind with stories I'd heard from ex-Immanuelites. They might have drawn from the same cast of characters: staid former brethren clashing with loud-shirted liberals; upper middle-class folk bumping up against working and lower middle-class.

When I asked my dad about Immanuel's early years, he said he used to turn up with one or two of his poems in his notebook. If the moment felt right, he'd share one during the worship. He'd feel, in the wake of the poem, the energy of the room change. The course of the service would shift, prompting others to share – songs, visions, stories of their lives that week. Each offering shaped the way the meeting unfolded. As the church grew, the order of service became slightly more regulated. It remained true that in Immanuel, to attend the church was to be the church. It was shaped by your presence and you, in turn, were shaped by it.

I didn't recall ever hearing the word restorationist at Immanuel. For all the talk of historical movements – past outpourings in Scotland, Wales and the US; the underground church of Watchman Nee in Communist China – we learned nothing about the early days of the movement that spawned us. It was natural, perhaps, that in this collective flow state, we were less interested in what lay upstream.

On the line graph, the horizontal axis marked the passing of time. It started in the first century with the Day of Pentecost, and finished with the Second Coming. The graph was published in 1983. The section passing into the future was vague, lacking any dates, but there wasn't much of it. Judging by the trajectory, the world was due to end some time around the year 2000.

The graph appeared in *Restoration* magazine, the official mouthpiece of the movement, as an illustration of the restorationist view of history. When I first came across it, reproduced in *Restoring the Kingdom*, I stared at it for ten minutes straight.

The vertical axis showed the level of anointing: the extent to which the Holy Spirit was manifest in the worldwide church. It was fairly high in the first century, but the line dropped sharply as the church fell into error. It reached its nadir in 600AD, flatlining for a period of

900 years, labelled the 'DARK AGES OF CHURCH LIFE'. It started rising again at the time of the Reformation, its steady climb annotated with names of movements. These were the groups that were getting closer to the kind of church that earned God's favour: the Methodists and Moravians in the eighteenth century, the Salvation Army and Brethren in the nineteenth; the Pentecostals and Charismatics in the early twentieth. The Restorationists came last.

The level of anointing kept rising steeply as it passed into the near future of the late twentieth century, when the Restored church was expected to spread around the world. The line reached New Testament levels then surpassed them. 'RETURN TO FULLNESS,' said the annotation. Beyond this, a star appeared, labelled: 'JESUS RETURNS – RESTORATION OF ALL THINGS!'

I knew this story from my conversations with Dan. This was the vision which drove the most radical revivalists, the Latter Rain teaching that he'd pursued in his year out before joining SCOAN. I'd gathered, from speaking to a few ex-Immanuelites, that this was the kind of fringe teaching that had come into the church during the Toronto Blessing years. Reading Walker's book, I realized that the idea was anything but peripheral. It was the prophetic vision that restorationism was formed around.

Presenting the graph, Walker noted bluntly that no serious scholar would recognize the restorationist view of church history. The graph seemed accurate in at least one respect. It was a graphic depiction of what it must have felt like to be a first-generation restorationist.

When the restorationists read Paul's letters, in those heady early meetings in the London School of Economics, they were not eavesdropping on historical conversations.

That intimate voice was addressing them directly, across centuries of muddled obscurity. Paul was always in the business of collapsing time. A Jewish scholar steeped in the Hebrew Bible, he demonstrated in his letters to the early Christians how these ancient scriptures spoke directly to their own lives, predicting the life and death of Christ and His supposedly imminent return.

What had kept Jesus from returning, the Restorationists believed, was the Church's deviance from the principles outlined in Paul's letters. Paul's message to the early church was also a message to them. That which was foretold has come to pass, but only in part. The rest is up to you.

I remembered Arthur Wallis' dust jacket photo from the book table at the back of the Assembly Room. His appearance – thin, bespectacled and stern-looking in black and white – contrasted with the title of his classic work: *Radical Christian*. He died in the late 1980s, before I was old enough to pay attention. I never read his work in my Immanuel days, but had a vague sense of his status as a forefather of the church.

It was Wallis, according to Walker's book, who helped capture the energy of the London Brothers' early meetings and channel it into a movement. He'd started out in the 1950s as an itinerant preacher, gaining modest renown for a 1956 book on revival. He'd got to know a number of London Brothers on his travels around the UK in the 1960s. By the time of the legendary meetings of the London Brothers at the LSE, he'd become convinced that they were central to God's plan for the church, but he was cautious. He believed that the things he'd witnessed in earlier decades – Pentecostal revivals, charismatic movements within traditional denominations – were genuine moves of God. The blessing, he believed, had been squandered, pressed into the service of sectarian gain. The churches had failed to realize that God was demanding a more radical change.

He brought together a small group of the London Brothers to discuss his vision. Their task was to find a way of doing church that was stripped back, spirit-filled, and radically true to scripture. At first there were six of them, but one, a charismatic Welshman called Bryn Jones, had a prophetic word: 'Seven shall you be, and thrice shall you meet.' They decided on a seventh brother to make up the numbers. They half-jokingly dubbed themselves the Magnificent Seven. Later, disregarding Jones' prophecy, the group expanded, renaming themselves the Fabulous Fourteen.

Together, they formed a covenant with God, each promising to put the vision of the group over their own personal ambitions. They began to meet regularly to pray, fast and study the Bible together. An older American preacher, Ern Baxter, was a frequent visitor and important influence on the group. He'd once been an associate of William Branham, the renowned Pentecostal preacher and faith healer, who preached a similar End Times theology.

'It was He who gave some to be apostles,' wrote Paul in his letter to the Ephesians, 'some to be prophets, some to be evangelists and some to be pastors and teachers, to prepare God's people for works of service, so that the body of Christ may be built up.' The Fabulous Fourteen believed that God intended them to take up these long-neglected offices in the restored Church. They just had to figure out who was who.

They realized that they were already living out their ordained roles. In the preceding years, some had given prophecies that had been fulfilled. Others had planted several churches. Some had personally brought great numbers of people to Christ. They prayed, talked, sifted through the evidence, and agreed on each member's title. Apostle and Prophet, it seemed, were the highest status. Some people's achievements didn't quite translate into titles. They concluded that Arthur Wallis, the man who had brought them together, was not an Apostle as he hadn't established churches. Some of the leaders met criteria for both.

There were times when reading Walker's account of the Fabulous Fourteen made me want to pitch a sitcom. All this biblical grandiosity playing out in the semi-detached houses and hotel function rooms of the 1970s. The mix of sincere conviction and male ego. What did the wives say, when the men got back late on a Saturday night to their homes in Ilford or Cobham, and announced that they were Prophets? When the men complained (as they plausibly might have) that Bryn Jones, that sharp-suited, sports-car-driving miner's son, was both a Prophet *and* an Apostle?

There was an epic argument about masturbation, in which Gerald Coates, who believed that it wasn't a sin, tried to get the more puritanical brothers, outraged by its very mention, to admit that they sometimes did it themselves. There were trips to the US, in which they got a taste of the swimming pools and megachurches of their prosperous apostolic cousins.

The Fourteen never agreed on much, but what they did agree on was explicitly theocratic. They were working towards a world church in which believers willingly submitted to divinely ordained authority.

The story of the Fabulous Fourteen helped me understand a few things. For many modern Christians, a leader who proclaims himself to be a prophet would be automatically dismissed as a charlatan or a madman. Not for the restorationists. Their emphasis on these New Testament roles seemed to dwindle over the years; no-one, to my knowledge, claimed such titles in Immanuel. But for some older Immanuelites, TB Joshua's embrace of prophethood may have hearkened back to a bolder, more faithful time.

There was precedent, too, for SCOAN's authoritarianism. Many restorationists – though not all – followed the teachings of Watchman Nee, who was heavily influenced by the teachings of the Plymouth Brethren, a nineteenth-century Anglican sect. He taught that any rebellion against church leaders – God's delegated authorities – was rebellion against God. If such authorities commanded someone to sin, he claimed, God would not punish the person for obeying. To reject such commands as sinful would be to commit the greater sin of insubordination.

Someone cynical and calculating could endlessly exploit such authority. In the 1990s, Bob Jones from the Kansas City Prophets, an American group that had close links with Restorationist leaders, was dismissed from his ministry for using his 'prophetic powers' to solicit sexual favours from women.

The Fabulous Fourteen split up a few years after their covenant was made. Later, Wallis would speak of his regret that they'd ignored Jones' prophecy and expanded beyond the Magnificent Seven. The movement divided into two factions. One of the dissident brothers refused to submit to Wallis' authority because Wallis wasn't, like him, an Apostle. Wallis accused the rebellious faction of being led into deception by demons.

Their prophetic vision granted extraordinary energy

and purpose, but it exacted a cost. Everyday life became a sign of failure: the absence of miracles, the Messiah's stubborn refusal to return. Human failings and frictions were transformed into spiritual warfare.

I'd always assumed that TB Joshua was cynical to the core, but who knows? Maybe he was a true believer. Or perhaps at a certain point, the distinction breaks down. Maybe the deceit and cruelty of SCOAN was partly the result of years of pursuing his prophetic calling while frantically trying to hide – from others and himself – his human fallibility. In the film version of *The Wizard of Oz*, Dorothy and her companions return to the wizard having completed their quest, hoping that their wishes might be granted. When the wizard is unmasked as a fraud – a small man stepping out from behind his lever-operated contraption – Dorothy confronts him. 'You're a very bad man!' she says. 'Oh no, my dear,' he replies. 'I'm a very good man. I'm just a very bad wizard.'

Walker's book shook my sense of Immanuel as a reasonably sound community that was overtaken, some time in the 1990s, with a rogue strain of Christianity. Did the good bits of Immanuel only ever exist in service of this End Times vision? Was it a temporary microcosm of stability within a macrocosm of madness?

One evening, visiting my parents, I showed them the graph from *Restoring the Kingdom*. My mum took the book and squinted as she traced the line up through the centuries. When she got to the bit with the restorationists ushering in the Second Coming, she sighed.

Their beliefs had changed a lot from those days. They now attended a village Anglican church, and had become more liberal as the years had passed. They told me that they'd always been wary of this End Times talk. Dad remembered poking gentle fun at those who took it too seriously. Once, compiling a draft programme for upcoming children's meetings to be reviewed by the leadership team, he'd added a teaching session on 'pre-millenialism for kids'. Some people believed this stuff, they said, but not everyone. It wasn't what motivated Immanuel in the early days. There were things that Immanuelites achieved that were, to them and many other Immanuelites, intrinsically good: building and sustaining a church, helping each other, emulating Christ, seeing lives change for the better. The Second Coming was the furthest thing from their minds.

I remembered my conversation with Isabel, one of the earliest members, who'd left her Anglican congregation to join Immanuel when it was still a small house church. 'Of course, it was very fundamentalist,' she said. 'There were people there who were creationists, and I wasn't. I had some theological training – I knew that some of the things proclaimed were not quite right. But I put that to one side. My feeling was: no church is perfect, but people there were like-minded. They just wanted to serve Jesus. And that was what I wanted to do.'

I found a video online of Terry Virgo, one of the former London Brothers, preaching in the early 2000s. He reminisced about Ern Baxter and Arthur Wallis. He spoke about his continued hope for a restored church. I now knew that his message was pure restorationism. Everything he said – his imagery, his rhetoric, the tone and timbre of his speech – was intimately familiar from Immanuel. This kind of talk had been with us for as long as I could remember. This was prophetic speech that did not primarily aim to predict, or to present doctrinal truths with clarity. What it did was galvanize, encourage, edify.

120

It conjured a vague glorious horizon that we all marched towards, with our mundane works, our sacrifices, our worship. Some people believed strongly in the doctrine behind the speech. Some people doubted its central tenets, or took issue with the details. Many others saw it all as 'theology': something esoteric and trainspotterish, about which they knew little and were disinclined to learn more. We all glimpsed the glorious horizon.

It was not right to say that this doctrine united Immanuelites. The shared pursuit of its vision bore fruit, and Immanuelites were united in the appreciation of the fruit. For years, Immanuel Church worked. People built lives, forged deep relationships, found joy and purpose.

Would such all-out corporate commitment have been possible without such a radical vision? It's hard to say. It was not enough, though, to simply sustain this everyday goodness. The prophetic vision – at once a guiding light and a source of perpetual dissatisfaction – demanded its due.

Reading Walker's book, I soon realized why I'd never heard of restorationism back in Immanuel. It was a term favoured more by sociologists than church members. When your movement is founded on the rejection of all denominations, gaining a name can be fatal. The provisional or jokey titles that groups acquired – the London Brothers, the Fabulous Fourteen – were attempts to remain unnamed, to avoid falling back into the sea of -isms from which they had emerged.

Any group bound by a rejection of inherited tradition has its own midlife crisis built in. How can you settle down without betraying the spirit of the movement? And what do you teach the children? We never had the class on pre-millenialism, but by the turn of the millennium,

Dan and I had both picked up, in our own different ways, the defining spirit of restorationism. We freed ourselves from the fetters of our childhood church. We kept moving, and we didn't look back.

In the 'Prophecies' section of the church magazine, a visiting preacher brought a vision of a double-decker at a bus stop. The top deck was empty. People from Immanuel were sitting downstairs, and there was a long line of people waiting to get on. Many were sick, injured, in no state to climb the stairs. The conductor asked the passengers to make room, but some people refused. 'We're comfortable where we are,' said some. 'We've got baggage that's too heavy to take upstairs,' said others. The Lord was saying that He was moving people to a higher place, explained the preacher. Being dislodged might be uncomfortable, but God was doing it His way, not ours.

Late one night, Teresa left her house and drove to St John's. She let herself in the back door with the set of keys she held as church treasurer. She climbed the stairs, entered the Assembly Room and lay down in the darkness.

We were in a bustling café at the top of Winchester High Street when she told me the story. She'd agreed to come and meet me on her lunch break from her office job nearby. I hadn't seen her since she'd left Immanuel in 1998. She'd often come round for Sunday lunch before then. She always dressed in similar clothes: dark trousers and a plain green jumper, shapeless over her large frame, a self-imposed Treasurer's uniform to go along with the leather briefcase that was never far away. I liked her bluntness, her kindness and self-deprecating wit. I wanted to know what had made her leave.

She was never at home, she told me, with the fervour of the revival years. She'd heard the prophecies shared

at Immanuel that called out the lukewarm and complacent. She knew that she was not one of those dancing
in the rain, but it wasn't for lack of trying. She'd gone to
Toronto to experience the blessing at its epicentre. She
was amazed by what was going on there, but it hadn't
touched her. She'd tried to fake it, and she was no good
at that either. She blamed herself. She wasn't praying
enough, wasn't reading the Bible enough, wasn't a good
enough Christian.

That night, lying on the floor of the Assembly Room,
she called out to God. 'Either touch me,' she prayed, 'or
let me die.' She stayed there for a while. Every now and
then a bus would pass by, throwing light and shadow
across the walls.

Teresa laughed recalling it. 'Absolutely nothing happened at all,' she said. 'Except I got bored of watching the
buses pass. So I just thought. "Oh well. It was worth a try."
And I went home.'

She began to realize that the problem might not be
her. After almost twenty years at Immanuel, her exit was
quiet and swift. One Sunday she was there, and the next
she wasn't. When she told Pastor Graham she intended
to leave, he'd asked her to go without speaking to anyone – she supposed he was worried about the spread of
discontent. But she couldn't bring herself to walk away
silently after so many years. She called a number of her
closest friends and told them about her decision.

Teresa now attended a small Anglican church in central Winchester: a haven of stone and timber hidden
between shops and cafés. It was a better fit for her, she
said. She liked the meditative quiet, the sense of history.
Like in Immanuel, she managed the church's finances.
'It's good for me to be accountable, to be part of something,' she said. 'When I'm tired and don't feel like getting

up on a Sunday morning, I'll get up because I've got six cheques to collect.'

Craig asked what I was writing about. It was late. My wife, who'd heard it all before, left the conversation and headed to bed. We didn't see Craig that often anymore. When he was studying Oceanography in Southampton, we used to play music with him. He finished his studies, took a detour into macroeconomics for a few years, then moved to the US for a post-doc position in Climate Science. I savoured these rare chats with him, though we always stayed up far too late. Things would get dizzyingly existential; the kind of conversations that are hard to wrap up. Maybe it was the oceanographer in him. Whatever our starting point – work, love, faith, politics – we'd be pulled out into ever-widening gyres, and end up facing the apocalypse.

I started talking about Immanuel. I told him about the things I missed. About the strange highs of the revival years, the beginning of the church's involvement with SCOAN, and its painful decline and fall. I couldn't talk about the topic succinctly. When I broached it with friends, I could usually feel their attention draining as I spoke, as if I was recounting a bizarre and interminable dream. From Craig, I got a look of recognition. He told me that my story reminded him of the Minsky hypothesis.

Hyman Minsky, he explained, was an American economist who developed a theory explaining the instability of capitalist economies. He died in 1977, and remained a fairly obscure figure for years. It took the 2008 financial crisis for people to realize how prescient he'd been.

Minsky proposed that prosperous and relatively stable economies had a tendency to turn to increasingly risky, speculative forms of finance over time. When times are good, investors are drawn in by the reasonable expectation of a good return. For a while, growth is a self-fulfilling prophecy. And yet the need for ever-increasing returns on investment never lets up. Ever more precarious ways of sustaining growth start to emerge. After a while, the very constraints and regulations that enabled the original stability are cast aside or circumvented. The pursuit of this vision of unending growth becomes destructive, self-cannibalizing.

Maybe Craig was right. The revival era of the 1990s was a kind of sub-prime mortgage crisis of the church. I thought of Tommy Tenney's cries of 'More Lord!', the perpetual searching for the next great move of God, the increasing impatience with the strictures of community and pastoral care. Chasing this glorious future, the only way forward was acceleration.

It's worth saying that some churches that emerged from restorationism are still thriving. Southampton Community Church – of which Immanuel was initially a satellite – remains a major presence in the city. I wrote to the pastor requesting an interview but got no reply. Many congregations – judging from online discussions and articles – moved away from the more extreme teachings. Immanuel was not unusual. Of the international disciples who went to Lagos to serve TB Joshua, many were from other British churches that espoused the same revivalist teaching.

It turned out that the phantom revival of the 1990s was far from the first. High-profile preachers linked to restorationism predicted a revival in Wales in 1983 and in London in 1990. Forerunners of the movement like William Branham had prophesied earlier revivals, earlier second comings. We'd been trying to outrun our disappointment for decades.

The revival narrative we absorbed in the Toronto Blessing years promised all the excitement of the apocalypse without the downside. It was a Michael Bay kind of Armageddon: awesome explosions everywhere, but barely any blood.

Revivalist Christianity was always a transatlantic movement. I remembered the preachers just in from the US or Canada, the Hollywood glamour of the accent, the jokes about jetlag and anecdotes about sharing the Gospel with strangers on the plane, the stories of incredible moves of God *over there* that were about to come *over here*. Recently, I came across a '90s YouTube clip from Toronto Airport Fellowship in which the preacher said he'd just come in from 'the revival in London'. In Immanuel, we'd never been told about a revival happening in London – if we had, we'd have got the train up there. I realized that the transatlanticism worked both ways. The power was in the distance: the glimpse of something just out of reach.

I was entirely ignorant, as a teenager, of the politics of the US revivalists. For the most part, they sat firmly on the political right, in a way that British restorationists never did. They were entrepreneurial men of God, who evangelized as fervently for unfettered capitalism as they did for biblical values. Their dismay at the immorality of the modern world sat alongside a whole-hearted endorsement of the individualist, consumerist status quo.

British restorationism shared with its American cousins the same biblical fundamentalism, but it was less firmly aligned with politics, and its rejection of modern society was broader. It sometimes manifested in familiar, ugly ways: a hostility to feminism and gay rights, a demonizing of those with different beliefs. There were other aspects of capitalist modernity that were worth opposing.

Immanuel put me in touch with certain truths that

seemed as pertinent as ever for our wider predicament. It gave me a feeling for the quiet pleasures of steward-ship, and the work of being and sustaining a social body, fuelled by love and hope. An appreciation of the interde-pendence of the self: the way we are formed by our bonds with others.

But the End Times narrative of the revivalists was like a grotesque parody of the hubris of the age: a literal End of History, a fantasy of infinite growth ending in triumph. The US evangelicals' alignment with race-to-the-bot-tom politics and Ayn Randian individualism made sense. Why bother with care-taking, with attending to the wider whole, if we're heading for the Second Coming anyway?

THE GIFT OF HEALING

To get to Isabel's house, I walked down Winchester High Street, past the bus station and onto the Broadway, where the statue of King Alfred stands between the two build-ings – the Guildhall, St John's – where Immanuel had once met. From here, the walk was a well-worn groove, the body-memory of countless baptism Sundays: over the pelican crossing, down the narrow pavement, past the pub to where the buildings opened up to the river, and a footbridge crossed over to the grassy banks and weeping willows of the other side.

Isabel's place was a short walk from the baptism spot: a small, terraced house that backed on to the Itchen. I re-membered Isabel as a fairly central figure in the church. A teacher by profession, she sat near the front on Sundays and participated with a quiet authority. I'd found some articles in the church magazine in which she spoke pas-sionately about the Toronto Blessing. She'd left the church towards the end of the '90s and I hadn't seen her since.

127

She was older but unchanged: diminutive and neatly dressed, her short dark hair now greyer. She showed me her writing desk, her vibrant textile art hanging on the living room wall. She put the kettle on, and we sat in her conservatory to talk. I asked her what led to her leaving the church. She told me that the catalyst was a trip to Toronto Airport Christian Fellowship.

She went with Gavin and Susan Winfield. She'd been looking forward to the trip, she said, but when she arrived, there were things that made her feel uneasy. A couple of leaders, she said, had the air of con people. She shared her discomfort with Gavin and Susan, but they didn't agree.

I told her about the videos I'd been watching of the leaders at Toronto. There was a man in a cowboy hat who spent fifteen minutes at the pulpit giggling like a drunk while attempting to read a Bible verse. It was so grotesque, I said. So transparently phony.

'I am absolutely certain that people acted,' Isabel said. 'And there is a real problem there. Because it wasn't all acting. Because it changed me. It really changed me.'

I asked her what she meant. 'I would guess,' she said, 'that I was healed of some stuff.'

I'd always known Isabel as one of Immanuel's single women. As a child, I had a vague sense of these women as a kind of caste: as if their singleness was an expression of their essence, not just the absence of a partner.

'In Immanuel,' she said, 'they had very strict rules about "not being unequally yoked with non-believers". If you were single, especially a single woman, you were expected to give chapter and verse of your personal life to your house group leader. I embraced this in my heart – it wasn't forced on me. But I was not naturally a single person.'

128

Over the years, she met men that she liked, but since they were not the kind of men the church would have accepted, she never pursued relationships. Good, single, born-again Christian men were hard to find. Immanuel's own pool of bachelors was very small. More than ten years passed and she found herself stuck in this role that she hadn't chosen.

'Psychological and emotional healing is a hard thing to understand at the best of times,' said Isabel. 'But things had happened in my childhood. My dad died. We were homeless for a while. There were all sorts of traumas and insecurities. The control and the straightforward rules of Immanuel gave the sort of support that all that stuff had left me needing. I'd always felt that Immanuel was stopping me from falling over a cliff. After the Toronto Blessing – and from then on – I didn't need somebody else's boundaries any more. I became a lot less judgmental. I was more open, more independent, stronger spiritually. And after the bad experiences I'd had with men up until then, I felt able to go into a relationship.'

There were other reasons for wanting to leave. She was removed, without being told why, from her role as leader of the prayer group. She was getting tired of the power struggles wrapped up in the language of prophecy and discernment. 'But what pushed me over the edge,' she said, 'was meeting a bloke. It was obvious that I couldn't be with him and be in Immanuel. I thought, "This is something I've wanted forever. I'm going to see where it goes."'

'We were together for twenty-one years,' she said. 'He died two years ago. It was a very exciting relationship, but not a straightforward one. It had all sorts of ups and downs. We both brought so much baggage with us. But it gave me – and I hope him – so much. I now consider it to have been a precious gift of God to me.'

She started attending a Quakers' meeting soon after leaving Immanuel. So much was strange and liberating: the broadness of their conception of God; the way they held scripture lightly; the sheer lack of curiosity about her personal life.

In hindsight, she realized that she'd left Immanuel at a good time. It was before TB Joshua came on the scene. Before divisions deepened in the church. Before Pastor Graham was diagnosed with terminal cancer, then proclaimed healed at SCOAN.

In the magazines, I found a 1996 article by my dad about his struggles with the Toronto Blessing. 'A dangerous equation,' he wrote, 'kept echoing through my thinking: *When God turns up, something dramatic will happen. Therefore if nothing happens, God hasn't turned up.* This was a lie. It was a lie that was more believable every time a speaker spoke about the Toronto Blessing. I got more and more stewed up about the shallowness of the whole thing... When I heard people say "God moved in power" because several people got the giggles, I wondered if we were living on the same planet.'

I'd known that my parents had been sceptical about the Toronto Blessing. I was surprised by the brazenness of this dissent, alongside the revivalism that dominated the magazine at the time. One evening, visiting my parents, I asked them why they'd stayed in Immanuel for so long, when it was moving in a direction so counter to their beliefs. They told me that they'd stayed for the relationships. Their oldest and closest friends were Immanuelites. They'd hoped, too, that their presence in the church could be a positive influence. By 2002, they'd made up their minds to find another church. Before the meeting with Pastor Graham could happen, his scans came back. He shared the news on a Sunday morning. The cancer had spread. They decided that this was not the time to leave.

If you wanted one thing from religion, you might reasonably expect it to help reconcile you to your human limits. Your propensity to mess things up. Your mortality. You might want it to provide a vocabulary, a set of rituals, that let you apprehend these truths, live with them, see beyond them. But restorationists didn't do religion. In Immanuel, the very word was a pejorative. We rejected dead tradition and pursued something more vital. A side effect of this, it turned out, was that we were really bad at death.

The Book of Acts gives many examples of the early apostles healing the sick and casting out demons. From the beginning of restorationism, a belief in this gift of healing co-existed with a disagreement about how it might manifest. In the first meetings of the London Brothers, one of the leaders claimed to have the gift of lengthening legs. He first pointed out that someone's legs were of slightly different lengths – this was usually news to the person – then laid hands on the shorter one and massaged it until it seemed to match the other. Other brothers, judging by their reminiscences in *Restoring the Kingdom*, remained unconvinced.

In early Immanuel, praying for the sick was common. When people were liberated from emotional pain or past trauma, this was understood as the gift of healing in action. Some Immanuelites had stories of doctor-confounding recovery from physical illness. Most people seemed to live in the zone of uncertainty between two beliefs: God sometimes healed, and often didn't.

Many preachers outside of restorationism – most of them American – built lucrative ministries around their supposed gift of healing. Kenneth Hagin, a pioneer of the 'Health and Wealth' school of teaching, claimed that all sickness originated out of evil. God, he said, doesn't want you to be sick. If you have enough faith, He will heal any illness. His teaching combined a belief in the gifts of the spirit with the bootstraps individualism of a self-help guru. End Times revivalists like the Kansas City Prophets went one step further. They taught that as we moved towards the restoration of the true church, an elite group of leaders would be chosen, known as the Manifest Sons of God, who would be granted literal invincibility. Death itself would be defeated.

When Graham got ill, this kind of teaching had already taken hold among some Immanuelites. People were passing around Kenneth Hagin books. The Winfields were already organizing group visits to the Synagogue Church of All Nations, and Dan had recently become a disciple there.

The prospect of our beloved pastor's death was made more unbearable by the promise of revival we'd been hanging onto for years. What if his illness was not just cruel randomness, but demonic attack, intent on thwarting God's plan for us? Not a tragedy, but a triumph deferred? A small group of Immanuelites – chosen for their commitment to this narrative – were gathered by the leadership team to mobilize for the struggle ahead. They called themselves the War Council.

I wasn't around for much of this. Between Graham's diagnosis in 2002 and his death in 2006, I was studying in

Leeds. When I came home for the holidays, I managed to avoid church by working most Sundays. I never spoke to my parents about the fundamentals of faith, but we'd speak freely about aspects of church that we agreed on. The cruelty and perversity of healing theology was one of those things.

In phone calls and visits home, I heard about Graham's trips to SCOAN, his refusal of pain medication even as his condition worsened (taking medication, it was believed, would demonstrate a lack of faith). On a rare visit to church, I watched as a woman in her forties, a mother of two, gave a joyful testimony of her trip to SCOAN, in which she'd been declared healed of cancer. As an act of faith, she said, she'd cancelled her mastectomy. She lived for another year or two before the cancer took her.

For TB Joshua, the gift of healing had a get-out clause. When healing took place, it was testament to the anointing of the Man of God. When it didn't, it was testament to the lack of faith of the person, or even the community around them. In Immanuel, doubt became dangerous. My parents were begged to believe that God planned to heal Graham. If the whole church was not united in believing, the healing might not happen.

There was no time for complacency or rest. As Graham got sicker, a rota was put together to subject the cancer to a constant barrage of prayer. In the day, Immanuelites sat with Graham inside the house. At night, it was decided to keep it unobtrusive. The person on duty would pull up in the gravel drive of the house and pray from the car.

When we are dying, what is the best we can expect? To be held and comforted. To be surrounded by loving friends and family. To be fed, watered, to have all the mundane practicalities taken care of. Immanuel could do this stuff with its eyes closed. But people's eyes were fixed on a grander vision – one which had no room for grief or human finitude.

A few months later, I visited Isabel for a second time. We sat down in her conservatory again. She told me that she'd been surprised at what our conversation had stirred up. After leaving Immanuel, she'd had recurring anxiety dreams for years. In the days after our conversation, the dreams had come back.

Since our first visit, I'd been thinking a lot about what she'd said. Before, I'd been trying to separate Good Immanuel from Bad Immanuel. Talking to her made me realize how tangled the whole thing was. Her story had shown the dark side of the superorganism. Every Immanuelite willingly made sacrifices: paid tithes, gave their time. But some – the happily married ones, for a start – could be both fully Immanuelite and more-or-less fully themselves. For others, being part of this wider body meant denying the bits of their own self that didn't fit.

Do you think it's possible, I asked Isabel, to have the closeness and depth of community we had in Immanuel, without the judgement, the control, the sense of us-and-them?

She thought it was. In the Quakers, she'd found a community that was no less cohesive for its lack of dogma. The Meeting House was a ten-minute walk down the river, a large eighteenth-century building which used to be a rectory. There was a garden, a kitchen and a library. There was a small residential community there – some Quakers, some non-Quakers. A few flats were reserved for a social project which housed people who might otherwise be homeless. But there weren't a lot of young people. Maybe when we're young, she said, we're looking for something clear-cut and certain.

The certainties of Immanuel had a lingering power over her. For a while, she said, she could barely read the Bible. She'd start reading the New Testament and feel suddenly convicted of sin. She couldn't read the book for what it was. The words were overlaid with the interpretations she'd picked up from Immanuel, all judgement and righteous clarity.

One Sunday, years after leaving the church, she was in her garden when she heard the sound of singing. It was a song she knew – an old praise and worship chorus – and she realized that she recognized the voices too. Once more, she felt herself to be a terrible sinner and backslider. Just downstream, on the other side of the river, her old friends were gathered. Immanuel church raised its voice as one and welcomed a new believer into the fold.

As I left Isabel's place, an old memory resurfaced. When I was a fresher at Leeds University, I'd once gone along to a Quaker gathering at a local meeting house. I'd been attracted, like Isabel, to the broadness of their theism. It appealed to me now; Isabel had sold it well. Back then, it wasn't the Quakers' openness to uncertainty that had put me off. It wasn't even the fact that everyone else seemed half a century older than me, though this didn't help. The silence and stillness had made me fidgety, beset with itches I couldn't scratch. I toe-tapped and clock-watched my way through the meeting and never came back. When I got home from Winchester, I looked at the website for Southampton Quakers. Would it be different now? Was it time to find another superorganism to join? The congregation in the group photo radiated such mild-mannered wholesomeness that I could almost feel the old itch again. I wasn't ready.

A couple of years after my conversation with Isabel, I

did join a superorganism of sorts. My wife, M, gave birth to a daughter. In the past, I could have easily persuaded myself that I didn't want children. I regarded the parents of young children with mild horror: their harried, diminished look, the way they stood around in parks with food-stained tops, weighed down with paraphernalia: sippy cups, nappy bags, tupperware. After L was born, the desk on which we pursued our passion projects – my writing, M's Open University degree – became a changing table. I mourned the solitude of my early morning writing sessions. Parenthood tossed us around like a dog with a chew toy.

I was grateful for the moments of sheer delight alongside the stress and drudgery. These were less of a surprise than the quiet satisfaction in the drudgery itself. Sleep-deprived and unkempt, hanging out at the soft play on a Saturday as L explored, I felt diminished and extended, at once less alive and more alive than I'd ever felt before. As tyrannical as parenthood could sometimes be, one of its gifts was that it demanded neither originality nor excellence. You only had to turn up, to be a servant of the superorganism. To clean, to change, to soothe. To sing the nursery rhymes, or rather let them sing through you, strange immortal creatures that they are. To get down on your knees on the linoleum of the kitchen floor for the nightly ritual: picking up, one by one, the sweetcorn and the peas.

IV. BROTHERS AND SISTERS

I first experienced the phenomenon of disciple-speak in late 2010, in a rented lecture hall in Birkbeck college, around the corner from Russell Square tube station. A few weeks before, I'd read Dan and Kate's email announcing their reasons for leaving SCOAN. It had left me determined to see the Synagogue Church for myself, and the London branch – which would soon be closed – was only a two-hour train journey away. I sat in the hall as a tag-team of young, white disciples took their turn to preach to the predominantly black congregation. Each one strode across the stage, leading the crowd in a call and response, channelling TB Joshua in every move and phrase.

On my way out of the meeting, I spoke briefly to Dan's mum Susan Winfield, who was sitting near the back. I told her that I'd read Dan and Kate's email. I asked her if she was worried about Kate's accusations of sexual abuse, given that three of her children remained disciples. She told me that it was completely normal for every genuine move of God to face opposition. On the train home, I wrote about the service in my diary. Susan's cold, strained smile and the briskness of her speech brought the word 'brainwashed' to mind, but even then, I sensed the metaphor was wrong. Talking to Dan and Kate would confirm this. Nothing was scrubbed or removed. The blankness of disciple-speak did not reflect an absence. What was going on beneath its surface?

A few months after my visit, in the comments section of the TB Joshua Watch blog, disciple-speak was a common topic of conversation. What happened to people when they became disciples? The discussions on the blog shed some light on the question, but it wasn't until years

137

later, through conversations with Dan and Kate, that I began to get my head around it.

We knew that TB Joshua Watch had reached the attention of the Synagogue Church when the copycat blogs started appearing. First it was watchtbjoshua.wordpress. com. Then came Watching TB Joshua, Watched TB Joshua, and other variations. Apparently written by disciples, most of these blogs pumped out large amounts of pro-SCOAN content, as if to bury any unflattering search results in an avalanche of puff.

I'd started the blog in January 2011. I wrote a couple of posts that summarized the troubling side of SCOAN and linked to some existing critical accounts online. I sent an email to a number of old church friends with the link. Soon after, my brother Ian offered to help out. He was a practising Christian, so could address theological issues with more authority than me. He was also better with technology. He overhauled the website, set up social media accounts, wrote posts on idolatry and healing theology. The daily visits rose into the dozens, then hundreds, and eventually thousands. Lots of people were googling TB Joshua.

The blog was, according to the counter-blogs, founded by former disciples engaged in a bitter vendetta against the Man of God. It was a reasonable assumption, but besides not being an ex-disciple, my own interest in TB Joshua was limited at the time. I was repelled by him, and wanted more people to know he was a charlatan. This was an odd, accidental hobby rather than an all-consuming passion. The blog brought its own rewards. It was nice, for one thing, to have a shared project with Ian. He was one year older than me, but our lives had diverged: he'd got married young, had two kids and moved abroad for work. We'd always got on well, but we rarely got around to talking without an excuse. We set up alerts to keep on top of SCOAN-related news. We sent ideas for articles to each other, and edited each other's drafts.

We learned that TB Joshua's notoriety extended beyond his claims of healing. His prophecies often made headlines. In 2012, he prophesied that an African head of state would die within sixty days. In a later video, he appeared to name a specific date. When the Malawian president, Bingu Wa Mutharika, died of a cardiac arrest on this day, he was succeeded by Joyce Banda, a devotee of TB Joshua who'd visited the Synagogue Church several times. In the Malawian press, there was speculation as to whether Joshua's prediction was coincidence, divine anointing, or some kind of insider knowledge.

Many of the prophecy videos were easy to debunk. Whenever there was a major terrorist attack, plane crash or celebrity death in the news, Emmanuel TV would release a video – clearly heavily edited – in which Joshua appeared to predict the event during a church service. By watching the footage of the full service, often available online, we could find the bits that had been cut: the details that deviated from the event that TB Joshua claimed to foresee. These prophetic patchworks were created with such efficiency that on one occasion, a single prophecy was chopped up to make two different videos, each with its inconvenient bits removed: one claiming Joshua had predicted a flood in Indonesia, another a typhoon in the Philippines.

In the comments sections of the posts, a cast of regular characters emerged, often writing under pseudonyms. There were a number of ex-Immanuelites. There were wives worried by their husbands' obsession with TB Joshua, and concerned friends and relatives of disciples.

There was Mr Terrific, a passionate and foul-mouthed critic of TB Joshua who'd been involved with SCOAN in Ghana. There were a number of former disciples. Some, like Dan and Kate, were thoroughly disenchanted. A few were more ambivalent, their comments wrestling with contradictions. 'Doesn't God move through imperfect vessels?' wrote one. Another regular ex-disciple, writing in a broken English that was hard to place, veered from acute insight to florid delusion, from scepticism to credulity, as if she was still only half-free from TB Joshua's spell.

I'd go on the blog a dozen times each day, checking page views, moderating and responding to comments. I'd sit in a café and work on posts before work. What made it fun was the sense of amateur sleuthing, the attempt to figure out how SCOAN worked. With the help of regular commenters and contributors, we wrote about the deceptions of the healing ministry, about SCOAN's ways of making money from visitors, like the 'free gift' of anointed water given only to those who'd bought expensive merchandise or otherwise contributed money. The relative ease with which these mysteries were solved raised another, more profound question. What kept disciples faithful to a ministry that relied on such crude deceit?

Discussions in the comments section were joined by SCOAN supporters. Some were trolls, damning us to hellfire in all caps. Two regular names, writing in what seemed to be Nigerian-inflected English, defended SCOAN persistently but more or less respectfully. Another, a self-described disciple going by the name of Radicalised, was more elusive, writing a comment then disappearing, ignoring follow-up questions. I spoke to Ian about Radicalised. They had a Lagos IP address, and clearly had inner knowledge of SCOAN. They also seemed to know who we were. We were certain that he or she was an ex-Immanuelite, though had no way of knowing which one.

The presence of Radicalised was exciting. If disciples were commenting, this meant they were probably reading the posts. Perhaps the pressures of church life made it easy to turn a blind eye to troubling facts about SCOAN. On the blog, they were all collected in one place. There was proof of fraudulent prophecies. There was a clip from Emmanuel TV of children singing a song of praise to TB Joshua – 'everything about him is good'. There was another of a SCOAN attendee calling TB Joshua the 'Jesus of Today'. It was difficult to imagine how anyone raised as a Christian could see all this, and not have their faith in SCOAN shaken.

'The first thing you do when you arrive as a disciple at SCOAN,' wrote Giles, 'is get shown your bedspace. The males and females are accommodated in two huge separate rooms full of bunk beds. You could fit at least fifty beds in each room. Ablutions would be six toilets, six showers and a couple of sinks. Your luggage would have to fit in any way you could – under the beds, in between the beds or in my case, along the one side of the mattress while I slept on the other side.'

Giles appeared in the comments sections of the first few posts, a British ex-disciple with a good eye for the detail of disciple life. When we emailed him asking if he would write something longer, he obliged. He wrote about the correction meetings, in which disciples would report each other for missteps. He wrote about *addaba* – the state of ostracism imposed by TB Joshua if an accusation stuck. He wrote about his experience of being kicked out of SCOAN. In 2006, after being granted leave to attend a family reunion, he was denied an invitation to return. He called all the numbers he knew, wrote emails asking to be allowed back, but was met with silence. 'I was living in the south of London in a flatshare where everyone seemed to get drunk and high all the time, working in a minimum wage job,' he wrote. 'So, I ended up doing what most guys would have done if they didn't know what to do with their lives. I joined the Army.'

Giles' rejection by TB Joshua didn't shake his belief that he was a great Man of God. When Giles was a disciple, his mum was diagnosed with cancer. She'd gone to SCOAN, where she was proclaimed healed. She'd refused chemotherapy but had kept getting sicker. When he visited her after leaving SCOAN, he sprayed her with TB Joshua's anointed water. It was only in Afghanistan that TB Joshua's hold on him began to slip.

After joining the Royal Engineers, Giles was sent to Helmand province, where a massive operation was underway to recapture Taliban-held territory. He was a sapper in the Counter-IED Task Force. His unit's role was to move out ahead of the advancing troops, identifying and destroying IEDs. He brought a bottle of anointed water with him, and sprayed everyone in his unit at the beginning of the tour.

His mum died when he was in Helmand. Two close friends in his unit were killed by roadside bombs. 'Turns out anointed water isn't IED-proof,' he wrote. During this time, Giles read the Bible every day. He'd wake up reciting psalms out loud – *though I walk through the valley of the shadow of death, I will fear no evil, for you are with me*. He realized that the love and solace he felt from these words was unlike anything he'd known at SCOAN.

Giles' account initiated a new phase in the blog. Other ex-disciples came forward, and wrote testimonies of their own experience. The blog became more than just a catalogue of TB Joshua's dodginess. Some days it felt like a spontaneous community, a place in which people could talk about experiences that had been life-changing, sometimes traumatic, but too bizarre for most people to understand. In the comments section, a mixture of ex-disciples and outsiders attempted to make sense of things that seemed, to me and many others, incomprehensible. What was it that kept people in SCOAN for so many years, in spite of the privation, the absurdity and abuse?

Giles' story contained a fascinating specimen of disciple-speak. Towards the end of his tour of Afghanistan, he began to receive emails from a disciple called Angela. The Synagogue Church, after ignoring him for years, was suddenly keen to make contact again. In Angela's first email, she warned him to dismiss any accusations he might hear from Dan and Kate, who'd recently left the church. 'I just want to tell you that the allegations are all false – there is no truth in them. You should not allow it to disturb you but treat it as the rubbish it is and discard it.'

Giles waited until he'd left Afghanistan before replying. 'I still don't know why my opinion is so important,' he wrote. 'I'd been told to leave when I was a disciple, and ostracized until I did. No-one was interested in contacting me or my brother when my mum was dying and we were trying to get through. No-one seems to be interested in the fact that I have just spent the last six months fighting in Helmand, and am now trying to adjust to normal life. No-one is interested in Kate and Dan's welfare either. All the phone calls and emails I've been getting are to do with defending the ministry's honour and winning people back to SCOAN.'

The disciple's reply came a few days later:

Hi Giles,
The internet here is a bit crazy and not consistent at all!
Hope things are going well on your end. Just wanted to
encourage you to examine all things in the light of God's
Word. Remember, we all came to Lagos because we wanted
to learn God's lifestyle – not that we live it already. If we
behaved perfectly, acted perfectly, reacted perfectly, why
would we want to go to Lagos to study God's Word and
character? We are all coming from somewhere – but by
God's grace we will become who God says we are.
    Sister Angela

What was puzzling about disciple-speak was how inef-
fective it was at persuading, or communicating anything
of substance. The slightest display of empathy or ac-
knowledgement – sincere or otherwise – would have
surely done more to reassure Giles. But this jumble of
pre-fabricated phrases, delivered with a vacant cheeri-
ness, had a chilling effect: like being visited by something
not-quite-human.

Disciples didn't pick up this way of talking overnight. In
his early months at SCOAN, Giles' commitment to the
ministry co-existed with a certain independence of mind.
'I've always been a bit gobby,' he told me, in a later conversation. He was often criticized by a number of zealous
female disciples, Kate and Mary Winfield among them. It
struck him as phoney to call them sister, he wrote, 'unless
I feel loved like my real sister loves me'. He called them by
their first names only, and for a while, he got away with it.
Dan also described feeling uncomfortable about the way
people called TB Joshua 'daddy'. He resisted using the

word himself at the beginning – though it was explained that this kind of thing was normal in Nigeria. *Addaba* changed everything. The unpredictability of the attacks in disciple meetings, and the pain of the public shaming that followed, meant that disciples looked for easy ways of staying relatively safe.

Giles' first stint in SCOAN came to an abrupt end because of a kitchen dispute. Unknown disciples had been drinking from his bottle of chilled water in the communal fridge and putting it back empty. He left a note on the bottle: *Don't drink! Contains my yucky saliva!* The bottle disappeared, then the note appeared in a disciple meeting, wielded by a disciple as evidence of Giles' bad behaviour. TB Joshua was outraged. The other disciples latched on to his disapproval, directing a litany of other complaints against Giles. Even the previously friendly ones added their own accusations. He was called to see TB Joshua after the meeting, who told him to pack his bags and leave.

When, after much pleading in the weeks that followed, he was given a second chance and invited back to Lagos, he decided to do it right. He called everyone sister and brother. He learned to deliver TB Joshua-approved teaching. He peppered his everyday conversation with Quotable Quotes, the words of TB Joshua that they were made to study and memorize. The change was dramatic. People used to leave the room when he entered. Now they welcomed him into conversations. He was given responsibilities: the youth work, the newcomers' department.

Giles learned that speaking like a disciple was as much about what he didn't say. Disciples couldn't criticize the prophet or SCOAN in any way, but it was also taboo to speak of any other Christian leaders favourably. Conversations about seemingly innocuous topics were also out of bounds. He recalled how as a new disciple, he'd ask others about their family, their hobbies, their churches back home. He was met with stern responses: 'That's not important.' 'I do not discuss my past.' Later he understood. Life at SCOAN was about pressing forward. Such small talk was seen as unserious. They were there to serve God, to learn from their mentor TB Joshua.

Giles' discomfort at addressing fellow disciples as 'brother' and 'sister' revealed a deeper truth about SCOAN. It was precisely those fraternal, horizontal bonds that disciple-speak denied them. People would spend years living together – sharing meals and dorm rooms, travelling the world – and yet barely know each other.

During Dan Winfield's first year as a disciple, his mum and aunt Madelaine came to SCOAN for a week, along with a group of British visitors. At the time, foreign groups would be given a short talk by TB Joshua early in their visit. This time it was different. TB Joshua had called Dan into his office with two other disciples, and told them to deliver a talk based on his teachings. He'd given them precise instructions about how to introduce themselves.

Dan was first to address the group. 'My name is Dan,' he said. 'By the grace of God I am an evangelist-in-training under my Father in the Lord, Senior Prophet TB Joshua. Before I came to SCOAN, I was a sinner. I thank God for the life of my Father in the Lord, TB Joshua. Before coming to SCOAN, I didn't know Jesus, but now through my mentor I have come to know Him.'

Later that day, Dan's mum came to him in the computer room in a state of agitation. Her sister Madelaine had been concerned by what Dan had said. Dan had been

146

raised as a Christian, and had chosen to be baptized as a young teenager. He'd just denied his previous faith, giving TB Joshua all the credit for his salvation. Madelaine thought this was a sign that SCOAN was a cult. Dan's mum didn't know what to think.

Dan was taken aback. He listened to her, and gently tried to reassure her that it wasn't a cult. She calmed down. Several other disciples in the computer room witnessed the scene. One of them went to report him to TB Joshua. Soon he was called into the office. TB Joshua scolded him, saying his conduct was unacceptable. He stayed in *addaba* for six hours that day, but the suspicion lingered for far longer. It took him months to regain his position in the hierarchy of disciples.

Dan couldn't understand what he'd done wrong. He'd challenged his mum, after all, and successfully reassured her. TB Joshua told him that he should not have even listened to such blasphemous words. Instead, he should have rebuked his mother harshly.

Disciples grew to feel no distinction between their closeness to TB Joshua and their closeness to God. A one-to-one relationship with Joshua was central to each disciple's life in Lagos. This was informed, in part, by beliefs that preceded their discipleship. Like Dan, many Western disciples came out of a Christian tradition which taught that, through baptism of the Holy Spirit, certain believers could reach a higher level of anointing, becoming a vessel for awesome acts of God. They believed that this anointing could be passed on from person to person. But disciples' relationships with TB Joshua were shaped over time, engineered by their experience at SCOAN.

Several disciple testimonies on the blog described first encounters with TB Joshua. Each story was near

identical. Foreign group visits to SCOAN were organized tours that followed a fixed pattern. Each one lasted
a week, culminating in a Sunday Service, then an individual meeting with the prophet for each visitor. They'd
spend days immersed in the sensory overload of SCOAN:
the crowds, the music, the healings and exorcisms. 'I was
hungry for more,' wrote a disciple known as Hattie. 'I remember reading the Book of Acts in my dormitory bed.
My experiences were shedding a whole new light on my
faith.' They'd watch TB Joshua from a distance, in person
and on video. They would come to the end of the week
feeling that he was anointed, chosen by God. At the end
of the week, in the one-to-one meeting in his office, they
would feel singled out by TB Joshua.

'He was kind to me, called me his daughter and gave
me privileges beyond what any other visitor would receive,' wrote Beth, another former disciple, describing
this meeting. Many disciples were left with a conviction
that their relationship with TB Joshua was unique: they
were unlike the others in some way, more highly prized.
In my conversation with Dan, he also mentioned his
special treatment from TB Joshua. When I pressed him
on the details, he mentioned a certain kind of chocolate
biscuit that TB Joshua knew he liked, and would occasionally give him as a treat. He laughed, and seemed
dismayed by the admission.

At SCOAN, nothing happened without Joshua's favour. There was no delegating. Most daily tasks required
permission from the prophet. Giles described the mob of
disciples that would form outside TB Joshua's office, all
waiting for him to sign a scrap of paper which served as a
permission slip for any number of tasks: checking email,
using the treadmill in the gym. Even when disciples were
abroad, TB Joshua would be in close contact with each

one, calling them on their mobile, giving errands, asking them questions. His attention and favour were scarce resources, for which they competed with every other disciple. At the slightest misstep – often impossible to foresee – his favour turned suddenly and shockingly to rejection and rage.

Beth, a British disciple who stayed in SCOAN for a year, recalled seeing female disciples heading to TB Joshua's office in the middle of the night and not coming out for hours. 'I never questioned it,' she wrote. 'In fact – and I'm so ashamed of my blindness – I felt jealous of the extra guidance they were receiving.'

TB Joshua encouraged distrust among the disciples. 'God has allowed snakes among us,' Giles recalled him saying, 'to sharpen up the good ones.' No relationships were more suspicious, in TB Joshua's eyes, than those of relatives. He emphasized Bible verses that encouraged leaving old relationships behind. In the Book of Kings, when Elisha first decides to follow the elder prophet Elijah, he asks permission to first kiss his father and mother goodbye. Elijah, seeing this as a lack of commitment, sends him away. 'No-one who puts a hand to the plough and looks back,' Jesus taught in the Gospel of Luke, 'is fit for service in the kingdom of God.' Being at SCOAN entailed a single-minded pursuit of God, and the way to receive God's anointing was through TB Joshua. The relationship with TB Joshua soon became the only relationship that mattered.

Disciples learned to dread visits from family, during which trouble was almost impossible to avoid. Dan was punished for not being harsh enough to his mother. Kate told me that speaking harshly to her mother came more naturally to her, but she got in equal trouble for precisely

149

this. 'So how did you talk to your family?' I asked them both.

Kate gave a demonstration. She spoke fast, all smiles. 'Hi! Nice to see you! How are you doing? Ah, that's great! You know what, I'll come find you later and you can tell me all about it – I've just got to go and do something!' 'There was always some job to run off to,' added Dan. Kate continued. 'And it's lovely to see you and thanks for coming and BYE!'

It was an exaggerated impression, but the transformation was uncanny. This was the essence of disciple-speak. It was not sinister in itself. It was the voice of a pestered flight attendant on a busy flight: irreproachably smiley and professional despite being the very opposite of relaxed. Deployed towards close relatives and friends, it was a suit of armour. It precluded closeness, warmth, even familiar frictions and conflicts. It was a refusal to be drawn into any emotional bond besides the one with TB Joshua.

The more Dan's family got involved in SCOAN, the more stressful life got for Dan. His parents became important figures at the church, organizing regular tour groups from the UK, helping facilitate foreign crusades. But TB Joshua often complained about them to Dan, suggesting that they were profiting dishonestly from SCOAN. By the time Dan's younger siblings joined as disciples, he'd learned the dangers of showing warmth towards family. His sister Mary and brother Michael both came out in their teens, having quit their studies to become disciples. His sister Hannah came out a few years later, after graduating from university. Dan had always got on with his siblings, but each time one of them arrived, he made a point of treating them like strangers. He kept his distance, speaking to them politely but coldly.

'I knew I'd get in trouble,' he told me, 'so I learned to overcompensate.'

I'd always thought that Dan's whole family had joined SCOAN, but this wasn't true. A family had gone in, but the bonds that made them a family were the first things to be broken down.

A British woman in the comments section of the blog shared a story. A female friend of hers had died of cancer after being declared healed by TB Joshua. This friend's son had become a disciple at SCOAN. Speaking at her funeral in the South of England, he did not refer to her as his mother, but his sister. TB Joshua, he said, was their Father in the Lord.

In the photo, three disciples walk towards the camera, smiling. Kate, Dan, and Sean, a young South African of Indian heritage, are on assignment in Johannesburg. The sun is high in the sky. Their outfits are smart and coordinated: white jackets, coloured shirts. Behind them, the grand gate of a walled compound, trees lining the edges. Something about this ensemble of disciples – their confident stride, their snappy dress – put me in mind of the opening sequence of a heist movie: the gang is here, and they've got a job to do.

I'd been immersed in interview transcripts and blogposts when Dan and Kate sent me a selection of photos, along with a video taken in the same period. The disciples' accounts had left me with a sense of the gruelling alienation of life at SCOAN. The photos backed up the accounts of sleep deprivation, at least: in every other image someone is sprawled unconscious or red-eyed with tiredness. Elsewhere, I was surprised by the high spirits, the apparent camaraderie.

Why the surprise? They resembled what they were:

the emissaries of a millionaire Man of God and international celebrity. Their task in South Africa was to set up a base for broadcasting Emmanuel TV, working with a company called Telemedia. They were working out of a house in an expensive area of Johannesburg that TB Joshua had acquired through a wealthy South African benefactor.

In the video, Sean gives a tour of their Joburg HQ. The camera pans around an improvised office based around a large dining table, a whiteboard on the wall, full of logistical scribbling. Disciples work at various laptops. A tired-looking Kate, her head propped up on her elbow, lifts a mobile phone above her head so they can get coverage for a Skype call to Lagos. She laughs wearily at Sean's bad jokes: 'Skype.com? More like scrap.com!' One disciple has Emmanuel TV on screen. Another works on Photoshop. The camera turns to Dan, lying on the floor with his eyes closed. 'The life of a Joburg disciple!' says Sean, laughing as he goes in for a close-up. Dan pulls his white hoodie over his face.

We spoke about the photo album over the phone. They learned a lot on these trips, Dan said. He enjoyed being thrown in at the deep end, working through the night to make things happen. Dan was given the technical jobs. He learned to set up computer networks, create computer graphics for Emmanuel TV idents. Kate's responsibilities were on the business side: registering companies, taking care of finances.

In one of the photos, a young, bespectacled black man stands in front of a bank of televisions and a rack-mounted computer server. In the email, Kate pointed him out as a Senegalese disciple called Racine. 'He's a really lovely guy,' she wrote.

Later, in our phone call, I asked Dan how such fondness

could grow in such an environment. It seemed to contra-
dict what I'd heard about relationships among disciples.
'You have so many shared experiences,' said Dan. 'You
can never have a heart-to-heart with anyone or be completely open. But you can choose to spend more time with
someone, or ask one person for help instead of another.'

Racine was a good colleague – he was kind, patient,
competent. Their relative closeness was also due to a
loophole in TB Joshua's paranoid temperament. He was
most wary of pre-existing bonds. Disciples who spent
too much time with their own relatives would be quickly
punished. Relationships between compatriots were also
scrutinized and discouraged. Racine was a foreign disciple, outside of the Yoruba-speaking inner circle. The fact
that he was black, and neither British nor South African,
meant that the time Dan and Kate spent with him aroused
less suspicion. Their relationship remained superficial –
they knew nothing about his life before SCOAN – but
they were closer to Racine than many of the others because he didn't threaten their relationship with TB Joshua
as much.

The photo album showed a side of SCOAN I'd over-
looked. It felt good to be a superorganism. It must have
been exhilarating to work for a ministry that was expanding, attracting wealthy donors, filling stadiums around the
world, apparently favoured by God. For all the teamwork,
SCOAN was a strangely atomized collective, entirely
centred around one man. In many ways, individual selves
were subsumed into the whole – there was little room for
idiosyncrasy or choice. But the engine of SCOAN was
individualism. Each disciple was a God-chaser, pursuing
their own divine anointing through TB Joshua: relentlessly, tirelessly, unimpeded by any other bonds.

What does it feel like to be cut off from all bonds but one? It's hard to imagine, suspended as I am in a web of relationships so familiar that they often feel like nothing much at all: the rhythms and rituals of family life, the relatives and old friends whose company is a mild sedative, in whose eyes I know I am neither contemptible nor very impressive.

A disciple is untethered from all this. It is not just her sense of worth that is precarious, subject to wild swings between grandiosity and shame. Reality itself becomes unstable. The blindingly obvious is obscured. The most fantastical untruths are made plausible.

Kate gave birth to her daughter in 2009. At the time, she and Dan were living in London and running the UK branch of SCOAN. Moments after the delivery, TB Joshua called her on her mobile to name the baby. Lying in her hospital bed, Kate struggled to understand the name. After he repeated it, and eventually spelled it out, she was no less baffled. 'Loveth?'

Dan and Kate told me that they both privately hated the name. 'Apparently there are people in Nigeria called Loveth,' Dan told me. Kate looked at him sceptically. 'But *are* there? We've heard there are, but I've never met a Loveth.'

'We just had to make the most of it,' Dan told me. 'So we'd tell people, "Yeah, as in 'And God so loveth the world..." And people would be like "Oh wow, such a nice name!"'

At the time, neither mentioned to the other how much the name bothered them. One evening, Dan mentioned casually to Kate that if it had been his choice, he'd have called her Leah. Kate repeated the name to herself, testing it on her tongue, but the conversation went no further. To go against TB Joshua's word was to go against God.

Even after two years of marriage, they would never criticize the prophet to each other. This was partly for fear, not unfounded, of being reported. More than this, they believed, like many other disciples, that TB Joshua was omniscient, capable of reading thoughts and eavesdropping on private discussions.

Every conversation, whether with relatives, congregants, or a fellow disciple, was in part a performance for the Man of God. This accounted for the odd disconnect of disciple-speak. When a disciple spoke, he spoke past you, addressing a presence over your shoulder, who could find fault in anything but the blandest platitudes.

The testimonies on the blog were compelling, I realized, because they were instances of the very connection that was denied the disciples in the Synagogue church. In describing this strange state of aloneness, the ex-disciples were enacting its opposite. The sharing of stories was not just catharsis, but a kind of triangulation. To see things through the eyes of others was to see beyond the first-person perspective, distorted as it was by shame and yearning and the manipulations of the church. But there were limits. These conversations took place among people who, for the most part, had already made their minds up about SCOAN.

Radicalised continued to appear sporadically in the comments section. Speaking to ex-disciples and Immanuelites, we became more certain of her identity. She was Mary Winfield, Dan's youngest sister, who'd arrived at SCOAN in 2002, when she was seventeen. At Immanuel, she'd existed in the periphery of my vision, in the way that younger siblings of childhood friends did. I remembered her as a good-natured, intelligent kid: blond-haired and tomboyish, quietly non-conformist. I remembered her in football boots and shorts. I remembered her learning the electric guitar; I used to vaguely covet her Stratocaster.

About a year after the blog began, we wrote a post called 'TB Joshua for Beginners'. It summed up a number of the controversies about SCOAN, linking to older pieces. In the comments section, Radicalised wrote several lengthy posts. 'For the benefit of those stumbling onto this site in an attempt to find out about SCOAN,' she began, 'I will briefly provide some clarification/correction to the claims above...'

The words that followed were vehemently defensive of TB Joshua, disputing every allegation, but they were not disciple-speak, exactly. They were detailed, showing a willingness to engage with specifics. Many old Immanuelites and ex-disciples began to respond. Unusually, Radicalised stuck around for the discussion. There was an atmosphere of hope in the comments section. If Radicalised was willing to talk, then she might just be open to persuasion.

Dan Winfield's aunt, the one who first raised concerns to Susan about SCOAN, appealed to her niece. Giles spoke about his own experience, and clarified his reasons for leaving. I replied at length with my own take. Each attempt at connection added another large block of text. People gave analogies, shared anecdotes, pointed out logical fallacies, appealed to reason. It was a pile-on. A benevolent one maybe – fuelled by concern and righteous indignation – but a pile-on just the same.

I'd believed that the problem was an information deficit, to be solved by the skilful deployment of facts. Later, I'd come to appreciate the true knottiness of the situation. As long as TB Joshua had a monopoly on a disciple's sense of worth, the only tolerable way of dealing with doubt or distress was to throw oneself more fully into a life of devotion to him. It was a closed loop: the solitary pursuit of TB Joshua's favour could be at once the main cause of a disciple's unhappiness and her only relief from it.

Radicalised had come to the comments section with a job to do. She responded to a few of our points, but the conversation soon petered out, lost in a sea of pro- and anti-TB Joshua screeds. Her comments on the blog became rarer, then stopped altogether.

As the blog entered the first page of search results for 'TB Joshua', we started receiving emails addressed to the man himself. People must have come across the site and concluded, without reading, that it was an official SCOAN webpage.

'Dear Sir,' began one, 'I have been having dreams about you, teaching me how to heal people. Since then, I have been having dreams about me healing people. I came to the Synagogue at Ikotun but you were not around... Am I being called to ministry? And how do I know if I am? Really need a reply from you Sir!'

The emails were pleas for healing, prayer or counsel, and occasionally for money. Most were from Sub-Saharan Africa: Nigeria, Ghana, Zimbabwe, among others. Some were very brief: 'How can I build my faith without getting weary, I'm losing hope everyday.' Others were sagas in miniature: tales of orphaned children, traitorous husbands, wayward brothers, dreams of studying electronic engineering thwarted by poverty. Some included attachments: CVs or scanned diplomas, photos of those asking for prayer.

The emails told stories of precarity, dislocation and debt. They were postcards from a world with no safety net, in which professions and degrees failed to guarantee a basic level of survival.

'I have tried to save my family from this financial hardship by creating other sources of income but to no avail. I currently have another business (selling of houses and lands, sugar and oil). Man of God, please help me break through with this business successfully. My sisters and I rely on my meagre salary which does not even last us the entire month. As a result, my mum supports us from her little daily sales.'

How could one man mean such different things to such different people? The majority of former disciples who'd made contact with the blog came from middle-class, Western backgrounds. Like Dan, they'd come to SCOAN seeking deliverance from the ennui of comfortable modernity: that state of cynical lukewarmness engendered by what Tommy Tenney called 'the lollipop of prosperity'. Others, inhabiting different modernities, looked to TB Joshua for a radical Christianity equal to the radical uncertainty of their lives.

Reading these emails, I was struck by the bare fact of TB Joshua's psychological power. They didn't shake my conviction that he was a charlatan. But people's relationships with him, while entirely imaginary, were on some level absolutely real. How many human longings converged on him? He entered peoples' dreams. He rallied them on. He illuminated hopes of a better future.

It seemed wrong to receive these heartfelt pleas and not reply, but as TB Joshua Watch, we could offer nothing but disappointment. I wondered if we might send some vague benedictions, at least. We wouldn't impersonate TB Joshua exactly, but leave it ambiguous. It might have energized them, lifted them out of hopelessness for a day or two at least. Would its fakeness have negated its usefulness? And would it have been any more fake than a reply from the man himself, who did not, in fact, have a direct line to the Almighty? In the end, we only sent one reply, to an Ethiopian man in the US who was asking for healing from HIV:

Dear G,
Thank you for your email. I will pray for you. I would urge you to follow medical advice and take medication if at all possible. Be careful of those who tell you to abandon medical treatment. God does wonderful work through doctors. God bless and stay strong.

G's reply was short, and clearly unimpressed.
'I AM TAKING A MEDICATION BUT I WANT TO COME SO THAT GOD MAY DO MIRACLE THRO YOU CAN I KNOW HOW?'

What G didn't realize – and who were we to explain? – was that any power TB Joshua possessed had an inverse relationship to his proximity. That he worked best, if at all, as a distant beacon of hope. That he did the least harm to the ones who couldn't afford to come to Lagos.

¶ It started around two months after Kate became a disciple. One day she was summoned by a Nigerian disciple to see the Man of God. She was led up the staircase at the back of TB Joshua's office, past the kitchen where his private chefs cooked his food, and told to wait in an unfamiliar bedroom. She waited nervously. Finally, TB Joshua came in.

Over time, the room would become all too familiar. There was a bed, but she would never lie on it. The prophet would tell her to strip to her knickers and lie on the tiled floor. It was the same ordeal each time. He would lie on top of her with all his weight, then masturbate. Afterwards, he would instruct her to get dressed and go. She remembered the heft of his body, the cold tiles against her bones. He was doing this, he would explain, to help her. He said he knew that Kate's mother had a past full of sin, and a long list of ex-partners. He told her that the problem was demonic, and that she would inherit it unless he intervened. He mentioned the Bible verses – Elisha lying down on the boy on the bed – in which a similar kind of healing took place.

She was summoned more often in the evenings. She started spending evenings sat in the unlit corners of the main compound, reading her Bible, or notepads full of Quotable Quotes. She hoped that the disciple sent to summon her might not find her. If she was found, she could say she'd fallen asleep while studying. Despite her attempts to hide, she was summoned for around two years: sometimes in the middle of the night, sometimes during the day.

What happened in the room left her feeling filthy and confused. The mechanical strangeness of the ritual, so unlike anything she imagined sex would be, meant she could almost believe in its obscure necessity. She could

160

believe, too, that she'd inherited her mother's spiritual problems, but how much deliverance did she need? She tried hard not to think about it, throwing herself into the work instead. Being visibly upset would get her reported, even if she was silent about the cause. Every now and then, when she was reading the Bible or praying for visitors, the word adulteress would come to her mind with a rush of shame. Something about her, she thought, had made a married man act this way. She knew it was a sin, but if she couldn't confess, how could she be forgiven? And if she wasn't forgiven, how could the Holy Spirit work through her?

One day, about two years after her first visit to the room, the ritual was different. He penetrated her. It was painful, and she bled. Afterwards, the prophet said that God had told him that this was not her first time. The blood, he insisted, was from a boil on his penis. Kate's fog of confusion gave way to a fierce clarity. She knew that she hadn't had sex before. She knew that TB Joshua was capable of lying. She knew that whatever he said, what happened in the room was purely carnal. Looking back, Kate thought that he must have noticed the intensity of her anger that day. He never had sex with her again. In the months that followed, the old ritual recurred once more. Then Joshua proposed that Kate and Dan should get married.

It was on one of my last visits to Dan and Kate's place that Kate spoke about her visits to the room. We'd talked about the impact of it, the chain of events it set off, but not the thing itself. I'd been putting off asking. If there was a list of Things Not to Ask Your Friend's Wife About, sexual abuse would be in the top five. As Kate and I sat on the high stools around the breakfast bar after dinner, I asked the questions, Kate answered them, and Dan

161

busied himself in the kitchen in grim silence. When Kate stopped talking, Dan embraced her.

In an earlier conversation, I'd asked Kate what had made her finally trust Dan enough to tell him what happened, after three years of marriage. She corrected me. She was never planning to tell him. She was convinced he wouldn't believe her. She was planning to leave him. It wasn't the relationship with Dan that prompted her to break her silence and escape from SCOAN. It was her relationship with her daughter.

When Loveth was born, Kate and Dan were living in Sydenham, south-east London, in a flat owned by Dan's parents. They headed the small team that ran the UK branch of SCOAN from a shared office space in Southwark. Dan and Kate had more freedom and privacy than they'd had in Lagos, but even in London, disciple life did not mix well with parenthood. Dan and Kate often had other British disciples staying in the flat with them; TB Joshua discouraged disciples from living with relatives when they visited the UK. They relied on money from TB Joshua for their expenses. Loveth went to nursery three days a week, morning to evening. Friends from church looked after her on some of the remaining days, so Dan and Kate had more time to run the church.

By Loveth's first birthday, Kate already had thoughts of leaving SCOAN with her daughter. On her second birthday, a couple from church hosted the party; urgent SCOAN business meant that Kate couldn't attend. She remembered cycling across London at that time, praying that her chain would jam, that she would come off her bike and be dragged under a bus. She wanted to die, but she couldn't leave Loveth.

Before becoming a mum, Kate did everything she

162

could to suppress her anger for TB Joshua. Afterwards, she was angry on her daughter's behalf. She allowed herself to think the kind of thoughts she'd previously pushed away. SCOAN was a place where bad things happened. The life of a disciple was not a good life. Loveth deserved better.

On 10 January 2010, a huge earthquake hit Haiti, reducing vast swathes of Port-au-Prince to rubble. Within days, Dan and Kate received orders from TB Joshua. An international team would be assembled: doctors, nurses, engineers and humanitarian workers. A cargo plane would be chartered to deliver food and medical aid. 'Haiti has given me sleepless nights,' said TB Joshua in the following Sunday service. 'If it means selling my clothes, I'll do it. We are going to take care of the wounded, the sick, the hungry.'

Dan left for Haiti soon after. Kate stayed in London, where she raised funds, looked after Loveth, and ran the UK branch. For Kate, helping to organize this humanitarian mission was exciting at first, but there were things that left her increasingly sceptical about TB Joshua's philanthropy. She'd contacted a British charity who'd offered to donate several thousand tents to the Haiti mission. TB Joshua refused to use them because they carried the charity's logo. Rather than coordinating with other humanitarian work, disciples had spent huge sums of money chartering a private cargo plane. At great expense, they'd had it repainted and emblazoned with the logo of Emmanuel TV.

On the phone, she discussed these things with Dan, who shared her frustration. As usual, they laid the blame on other disciples. Privately, Kate thought differently. She heard TB Joshua's wild promises on Emmanuel TV

– the 500 Haitian orphans he would adopt; the permanent free medical clinic and community centre he would set up – and she was sure that he had no intention of keeping them.

While Dan was in Haiti organizing the aid effort, Kate felt increasingly stressed. Loveth had an ear infection and was grumpy and sore; the doctor had wanted to hold off prescribing antibiotics. In the evenings, after putting Loveth to bed, she had to stay up late operating a prayer line set up by US disciples. SCOAN supporters from the US would call her with their prayer requests. She was running out of money. She'd been trying to call TB Joshua every day but wasn't getting through. 'Daddy's not here,' the disciple would say. She'd been that disciple herself, covering the receiver with her hand as Daddy waved the call away.

Loveth's ear infection got worse. One day, fluid started leaking out of her ear: the eardrum was perforated. The GP surgery was only a twenty-minute walk away, but it was raining, and a plastic cover for the buggy was one of the things that Kate lacked money to buy. When they arrived at the surgery, Loveth was soaking wet, crying with pain.

Days later, Dan returned from Haiti. That evening in the flat, Kate broke down in tears. Dan approached her to give her a hug. She hit him with all her strength. 'Daddy is a liar!' she shouted. 'Daddy is a liar!' He held her, absorbing her blows. 'Don't say that,' he whispered to her. 'Don't say that.' She calmed down, and was left with a new resolve. She started to plan her escape.

One Monday morning in March 2010, not long after Dan had returned from Haiti, Kate sent him a text. He'd just dropped Loveth off at the nursery. She told him to meet her in Tabard Gardens on the way back. This was a small park a few minutes' walk away from their Southwark office space. She'd wanted to break the news to Dan in a public place. She didn't think he would harm her, but in the flat, he might restrain her, lock the doors, tell TB Joshua that she was trying to leave. The plan was to tell him, leave the park, pick up Loveth, grab a bag from home and take the first available flight to South Africa.

When Dan arrived, she was sitting on a bench. It was a mild, cloudy morning. Joggers and dog walkers passed by. Nearby, people worked out on the outdoor gym equipment. She told Dan she wanted a divorce. He was shocked. He asked what was wrong. 'We're not even arguing!' he said.

Kate told him that she didn't want to be part of SCOAN anymore, that she needed to leave. He started asking questions. 'What happened?' he said. 'Has someone done something to you there?' Kate said nothing. She'd once told Dan that another disciple had done something she'd never forgive him for: he'd forcibly kissed her during a SCOAN mission to Cape Town. There were other people in the house: when she shouted and struggled, the disciple had backed off.

'Even if it was another disciple, I won't report you,' said Dan. 'I won't say anything.' Kate stayed silent.

'Even if it was Daddy,' he said. At this point Kate started to cry. She told him about the room, the ritual, the years of self-loathing. Dan called the office to say that they were taking the day off. They walked circuits of the park and talked. They shared experiences that they'd never spoken about: times they knew they'd been lied to, times they'd been compelled to lie on the prophet's behalf. They went home, ate lunch and talked some more.

When I spoke to Dan about this day, I asked him if he'd doubted Kate's account at all. It seemed odd, this sudden turn-around after so many years of total loyalty to TB Joshua.

He told me that he'd also been silently struggling with SCOAN. His youthful drive for anointing was fading. He'd become less interested in TB Joshua's teaching and had been neglecting his study of Quotable Quotes. There were numerous other things that had been troubling him. A few months before, he and Kate had been asked to distribute a DVD attacking Bisola Johnson, the dissident disciple who'd also accused TB Joshua of sexual abuse. It was not the first time he'd heard such accusations – two foreign disciples, Cindy and Abigail, had left SCOAN after alleging that they'd been abused. Despite this, Dan had been able to dismiss Bisola as a liar. Still, he'd found the tone of the DVD repugnant – thirty minutes of character assassination, using Bisola's own 'confession' videos against her. He and Kate had refused to distribute it to the London congregation, blaming other disciples for its production. It had been getting more of a strain to keep up the belief that TB Joshua was a great and infallible prophet surrounded by a few bad people. What Kate told him made sense of so much. Not only the cruelties and manipulations of disciple life, but also Kate's deep misery, which had been so inexplicable to him.

Later that day, after talking for hours, Dan left to pick up Loveth from nursery. When he was on his way back, Kate called him from the flat. She'd been doing some research. 'I've found an article about cults,' she said. 'You've got to read it.' The article, which they read together that evening, listed 'ten warning signs that you're in a cult'. For years they'd defended SCOAN against the charge of being a cult, but they'd never read a definition. They went through it point by point. Authoritarian leader with no accountability – check. No tolerance for questions – check. Followers being constantly made to feel like they are 'never good enough' – check. SCOAN ticked nine out of ten boxes. They only had doubts about one item: cult leaders make it difficult for you to leave. Throughout their time in SCOAN, TB Joshua had told them they were free to leave. 'Just come to me,' he used to say, 'and I will give you grace to go.' They decided that night that they would leave SCOAN, but they wouldn't just slip away after so many years of service. They had to go back to Lagos and talk to TB Joshua.

By the end of the day, Kate was exhausted and over-whelmed with relief. She could hardly believe that Dan had believed her. She was shocked, too, by the force and clarity of his anger. Her own, great as it was, had been blunted by self-blame. She'd been convinced that Dan would feel betrayed if he found out, for keeping this shameful secret through years of marriage. Yet his anger was all for TB Joshua.

They decided to take the prophet by surprise. They bought flights on the SCOAN credit card. They forged an invitation letter and took it to the Nigerian consulate to get a visa. They arranged for their friends Mike and Polly from Milton Keynes to take Loveth for the week-end. Mike and Polly attended SCOAN UK, but hadn't lived in Lagos, and were not TB Joshua devotees. They told them they'd been summoned to Lagos, and asked them not to tell anyone that Loveth was with them.

Their flights would get them to Lagos on a Saturday morning, and out the same evening to arrive at Gatwick on Sunday morning. They bought back-up flights for the following day in case they were delayed. They hired a driver for a day. On the website, the driver hire company offered armed guards as an optional extra. They decided to be on the safe side: TB Joshua was paying, after all.

When they arrived at Mohammed Murtala airport early Saturday morning, the driver they'd hired was awaiting them at arrivals. His name was Malcolm. They introduced themselves, and told him they wanted to go to SCOAN in Ikotun-Egbe. He wasn't happy. 'If you'd told me that before,' he said, 'I'd have charged more. People have gone in there and never come out.' Kate tried to reassure him: 'TB Joshua knows us! It'll be fine!' They walked to the car, where the armed guard was waiting. Malcolm drove them to Chicken Republic, a chain restaurant not far from SCOAN. They ordered coffee and waited for TB Joshua to wake up. Dan called his number twice. 'Daddy's sleeping,' the disciple said. A third time, the disciple passed the phone over.

Dan and Kate had discussed how they'd approach this. They wanted to talk to TB Joshua face-to-face, but didn't want to risk entering the building. On the phone, Dan played a husband exasperated by his irrational wife. He told TB Joshua that Kate had been saying terrible things to him, that he didn't know what to think. He told him that he wanted him to talk to her, but asked him to come out to the gates. He didn't want her speaking to the other disciples. TB Joshua said little in response, and agreed to meet them outside the church.

They made their way down Ikotun-Egbe road, past rows of shops, hotels and roadside vendors. Arriving at the church, they turned off the main road, passing the hut on the corner where a team of armed policemen stood guard. As they drove down the side street, approaching the high metal gates of the staff entrance, they saw a crowd of Nigerian disciples gathered outside. The gates were open. There was no sign of TB Joshua.

Dan and Kate had a Plan B. If the prophet didn't come down, Kate would make a scene. While living at SCOAN, Kate had seen mentally unstable people turning up at the gates, screaming and shouting. To her surprise, TB Joshua had always come out to speak to them. He couldn't resist the drama. When their car stopped outside the gate, she wound her windows down. As disciples surrounded the car, she began to shout.

'TB Joshua abuses people! I didn't come here for that! All these years I've been here!' Dan still played the exasperated husband. 'Kate, it's OK, be quiet.' A number of disciples shouted back. The group was headed by two Nigerian women from the inner circle of disciples, known as the Emergency Sisters. Olajitan was middleaged, huge and broad-shouldered. The other, Yinka, was shorter, younger, and did most of the speaking. When the initial shouting match subsided, she asked Kate what she wanted. Kate said that she wanted TB Joshua to come down so she could talk to him. 'Ok, no problem,' said Yinka. 'He's coming, don't worry.' A moment later, the group of disciples left, heading through the metal gates into the arched side-entrance, then disappearing down a bench-lined corridor. They were left with the stony-faced guards flanking the gates, their green berets and automatic weapons.

Malcolm, the driver, turned to Kate. 'Stay calm,' he said. 'Nothing is going to go wrong here.' The armed guard sat quietly in the back seat.

'Don't worry,' Kate said in a quieter voice. 'I'm *supposed* to be mental. We have to put on this kind of show so he'll come down. Otherwise I'm very sane.'

'Sorry,' added Dan. 'We really appreciate your help.'

'Are you in first gear?' asked Kate.

The group of disciples returned. They had grown in number. Racine, the Senegalese disciple, had joined them, amongst others, but there was still no TB Joshua. A shouting match broke out again. Disciples were calling Kate 'mental'; Kate was yelling back. Yinka spoke in a more consoling tone. 'You will see him. He is here.' She told Malcolm to drive through the gates. 'Just come inside, right here, not far.'

Another disciple arrived. 'I've just come from Daddy,' she said. 'He says to meet him in the presidential room.'

'I don't believe you,' said Kate. 'When I get inside, you will hold me down.'

'Why would we hold you down?' said Yinka.

Dan joined in, no longer the exasperated husband. 'Do you agree that TB Joshua has a bad temper?' he said. 'Has he ever slapped any one of you or pushed you over? Now do you understand why we don't want to go into a private room with him?'

'TB Joshua had sex with me,' shouted Kate, 'and I need to see him now!'

Another disciple came out of the building and walked towards the car. He was holding a black plastic bag. Kate immediately knew what was in it. It was this kind of bag, holding wads of US dollars, that was often handed to esteemed visitors or sympathetic journalists when they left the church. For a moment she thought that the bag was intended for them, but the disciple walked to the other passenger door and gave it to the armed guard sitting in the back seat. He took the bag and got out of the car. It was at this point that Kate realized they had to leave. Dan was outside, speaking to Racine, getting things out of the boot of the car. She shouted at him: 'He's not coming. He'd be here by now! I'm leaving you here!'

The driver turned the car round to face the main road. Dan, ending his conversation with Racine, got back in the car and shut the door. As Malcolm drove down the speed-bumped side road, the group of armed policemen from the sentry hut moved across the road, blocking their exit. Malcolm stopped, and Dan got out. He walked over to the head of security, explained their situation and asked him to let them leave. The head of security spoke softly but insistently. 'If you *know* she is mental,' he said, 'why can't you let us bring her inside?'

'I believe everything Kate says,' said Dan. 'I know he takes girls up to his room.'

When Dan got back in the car, Malcolm told them that they should leave on foot. They grabbed a small bag with all the essentials – passports, laptops – and left the rest, then ran past the row of armed security. One of them seized Kate's arm, but she pulled herself free. As Dan and Kate ran out onto the pavement, they saw an *okada* motorbike taxi approaching. They flagged it down, and jumped on the back.

Dan and Kate told me about this last trip to SCOAN in one of our first interviews. I understood – and admired – the impulse to confront TB Joshua. But I was puzzled by what they hoped to achieve. They told me that they'd had a genuine hope that TB Joshua might react with contrition: admitting his wrongdoing, giving them grace to leave. Yet they were aware enough of his capacity for violence that they'd brought an armed guard. Dan had wanted to vent his anger: the man to whom he had dedicated almost a decade of his life had been abusing the woman he loved. He told me that he'd also packed a box full of plastic lanyards to drop off, in response to an email from disciples requesting office supplies from London.

'It wasn't a rational train of thought,' Dan had told me. It was hard to disagree. But it seemed to me that this muddle of hopes and motivations was not madness – rather a kind of doubleness. As if their disciple selves and their nascent, post-SCOAN selves were overlapping, in a state of glitchy co-existence.

Still, how could such a plan have ever succeeded? What would have possessed TB Joshua to come out and be publicly shamed? Even the best-case scenario – the amicable and honest talk – could only happen in a private room, not outside the gates, in front of guards, disciples, and passing members of the public. It was a big risk – to themselves, not to mention the poor driver – for a plan that was almost guaranteed to go awry.

They mentioned, in that first interview, that they'd recorded a video at the gates of SCOAN, but weren't sure if they still had the file. On a later visit, I asked again. Kate disappeared and came back with a chunky, dust-covered laptop, which she plugged in and powered up.

She found the file and we watched it together, pausing to decipher the conversations. It was the first time she'd seen it since she left SCOAN. The video was low res and shaky, an artefact of the early camera phone. We saw flashes of blue sky, palm trees, SCOAN's Disneyland-style plaster façade, the armed guards, the disciples crowding around the car. We heard Kate's theatrical shouts giving way to genuine panic. ('My God,' she said as we watched the video, 'I'd forgotten how Nigerian my accent was.') We heard the surprising calm of Malcolm the driver. 'Ah,' he said, in response to Kate's explanation. 'I think I understand what is going on.' Above all, my attention was drawn to the moment Dan and Kate's friend Racine came out.

Dan had left the car to get the box of lanyards out the

boot. The clamour of the argument with the emergency team had died down, and he turned to talk to Racine. 'Let's look at the ministry,' he said. 'You can't deny the deception, the lying. It's not just Kate, Cindy, Abigail. He said he's taken in 500 orphans – it's a lie. 10 million dollars in Haiti – it's a lie. He lies clearly – how do you justify that in the Bible?'

Racine's replies were not audible, but Dan was doing most of the talking. He spoke in bullet points. He knew that Racine would have seen and heard things in SCOAN that did not sit well with him, and was aiming at these areas of dissonance.

A moment later, Kate joined in. 'My brother,' she said, 'before God, I was an adulteress! I've been on the verge of killing myself time and time again. I don't have mental problems. I have to counsel people and pray for them. And I'm an adulteress!'

Watching this scene, it seemed to me that the showdown with TB Joshua was not the true purpose of the trip. Dan and Kate wanted to get through to other disciples. This could not be achieved by slipping quietly away. Nor could it be done by becoming enemies of SCOAN, going to the press, doing things they'd learned to expect those with a 'lying spirit' to do. This awkward and contradictory encounter at the gates – the anger and defiance, the futile demand, the delivery of lanyards – was their attempt at a middle way. The confrontation was good for one other thing. They had video proof of the last item on the cult checklist: they were prevented from leaving.

On the back of the motorbike, they told the driver to take them to the Sheraton hotel near the airport. They'd only ever travelled in SCOAN vehicles, but it was well known that *okadas* were the fastest way of getting around.

They held on tight as the driver weaved between trucks and cars, passing swiftly through traffic. Kate shouted at him to go faster. Along the way, Dan's phone kept ringing. Each time, he saw Daddy on the caller ID, and let it ring out.

The hotel road was closed to *okadas*; the driver dropped them nearby and they completed the journey by taxi. They booked into the Sheraton and went to their rooms, where they showered and ordered food and drinks, still wired with adrenaline. It was around midday. They'd booked a room so they could lay low in the hours before their evening flight. The manager of the airport was a SCOAN member, and they knew that the airport was the first place that TB Joshua's people would look for them. That afternoon, they called Kate's stepdad in South Africa, one of the few people who knew they were there. They called Mike and Polly in Milton Keynes to check on Loveth. They called Dan's parents but couldn't get through – they were on a flight. They attached Kate's phone to the laptop and uploaded the video of their encounter at the gates. Dan sent the video to his parents, with an email explaining why they were leaving SCOAN.

A couple of hours after checking in, Malcolm called. 'You're crazy!' he said. He had been held and beaten by TB Joshua's men. They'd demanded that he tell them which flight they were on, and had driven with him to the airport to look for them. 'They're waiting there now,' he said. 'I only just managed to get away.'

Dan checked them in online. Kate went downstairs to the hotel gift shop, which sold Nigeria-themed souvenirs and clothes. Using the SCOAN credit card, she bought a traditional dress: colourful patterns going all the way down the ankles, a matching headband. She bought an outfit for Dan, similarly colourful, with a matching cap.

174

Back in the room, they put on their disguises and left for the airport.

'It wasn't necessarily that we'd be disguised,' Dan told me, in response to my surprise at this descent into farce. 'It was more that we could blend in in a crowd.' When they arrived at the airport, there were no crowds to disappear into, but plenty of people who noticed them. Kids laughed and pointed, shouting *oyinbo,* foreigner. Others asked to take a photo with them. But TB Joshua's people were nowhere to be seen.

They realized they were late. In all the rush, they'd forgotten to change their watches to Nigerian time. The plane was already boarding. They hurried to security. There were no queues, and they got to the gate in good time. Passengers were just starting to board. As they waited to board, Dan called TB Joshua. He picked up. Dan asked him why he held them against their will. He told him what Kate had shared about the abuse. TB Joshua listened. He didn't challenge anything or deny anything. After Dan was done speaking, he replied: 'I'm disappointed in you.'

Dan and Kate boarded the plane, relieved to be heading home. As they were taking their seats on the right-hand side of the plane, three familiar faces caught their eye. In the central aisle, a few rows behind them, were Dan's siblings: Michael, Mary and Hannah. Kate and Dan knew at once that that they'd been sent by TB Joshua to follow them to London. The three of them looked away, but when Dan's sister momentarily caught his gaze, she raised her eyebrows in feigned surprise, as if their shared flight was a happy coincidence.

The plane from Lagos touched down at Heathrow early Sunday morning. Dan and Kate joined up with Michael,

Mary and Hannah on the way to passport control. They agreed to get a coffee and talk. The five of them sat in the Costa in the arrivals hall. Dan and Kate explained their reasons for leaving SCOAN. The siblings spoke about the miracles. The philanthropy. The inevitability that every great move of God will be attacked. The conversation stayed civil, but it quickly became circular. Dan and Kate could tell that the three of them had been prepped by TB Joshua before their departure.

When Kate heard them talk, she heard herself. She'd said the same things so many times, in the same defiant tone. Not long after Abigail and Susan left, Dan's uncle had met with the two of them. He asked Kate directly if TB Joshua had abused her. She had denied it without hesitation. Dan and Kate were on the other side of the divide now, but they could not reach back over it.

They spoke for an hour before they left Heathrow and took the underground to central London. Dan and Kate had one more job to do. They weren't really in the mood for church, but it was Sunday morning, and they were still the pastors of SCOAN UK, whose congregation knew nothing of their confrontation in Lagos. Besides, they had a daughter to collect. They got off at Russell Square and walked through the grounds of Birkbeck College and into the lecture hall, where Mike and Polly waited with Loveth.

Before the service began, Dan looked out at the congregants. He was fond of many of them. There were things he'd got from SCOAN UK that he hadn't got from Lagos. Besides the healing, exorcism, and TB Joshua-style preaching, there was a communal spirit that reminded him of his childhood in Immanuel church. The shifts at the local homeless shelter. The shared Sunday lunches at church – the tables full of home cooking, and pastries and crisps from the local Sainsbury's. He and Kate had decided that they would get through this last Sunday service without rocking the boat. He'd open the service, then let the other disciples handle the rest. Soon Dan and Kate would send out the email, have the difficult conversations, hear the old familiar accusations of blasphemy and demonic possession. It could wait a few more hours. Dan took the microphone, and cut through the murmur of conversation with the usual greeting: 'Emmanuel!'

After the service, Dan, Kate and Loveth took the train back to their flat. In the following weeks, the three of them would stay in the spare rooms of friends, then friends of friends. They would have to figure out where to live, how to make a living, how to write their CVs around the fact they'd spent a decade in a cult. There was one choice that came easily. They decided to change Loveth's name by deed poll. They would call her Leah.

¶ On Friday 12 September 2014, at around midday, a six-storey SCOAN guesthouse collapsed. Around three hundred visitors were staying in the building at the time. Many were having dinner in the ground-floor canteen. TV footage showed the aftermath: a dense tangle of twisted metal, ripped mattresses and bedsheets, layers of collapsed concrete floors. Weeks later, a final death toll would be confirmed. 115 people were killed, 85 of whom were visitors from South Africa.

Before the collapse, TB Joshua had been out of my mind for a while. I'd no longer been maintaining the blog; other writing projects had taken over my free time. Ian had remained steadfast, manning the social media accounts, re-publishing old posts and occasionally writing new ones. From time to time, I'd check the google alerts, and read about the latest disaster TB Joshua had claimed to predict. But I could barely muster up much outrage anymore. In the weeks after the tragedy, I was once again gripped by the news from SCOAN.

Two days after the guesthouse fell, the Sunday service went ahead as usual. TB Joshua explained to the assembled crowd that SCOAN had been attacked. He showed a video that attributed the collapse to a plane flying low over the guesthouse. Later, SCOAN would make the claim more specific: a mysterious plane fired an infrasonic weapon at the building which caused it to collapse. The video showed CCTV footage of the guesthouse, pausing to highlight the silhouette of a plane flying overhead, then unpausing. Seconds later, the building fell, engulfing passers-by in a cloud of dust and debris. TB Joshua claimed that this was a failed assassination attempt. 'Don't be scared,' he said to the congregation. 'You are not the target. I am the target. I know my hour has not yet come. Anything close to Jesus receives attack.'

If TB Joshua was distraught about the loss of life, he did not show it. He gave one concession to the gravity of the occasion. He proposed a one-minute silence in memory of the victims, whom he referred to as Martyrs of Faith. The dead, lying under rubble just a few metres from the auditorium, had not yet been counted. But they had already been co-opted into a minor supporting role in TB Joshua's personal mythology. The minute's silence lasted just under twenty seconds, and TB Joshua moved on.

Over the coming months, the church's PR machine pushed Joshua's explanation for the collapse. Paid-off newspaper reporters spoke unquestioningly of infra-sonic weapons. (One brave journalist, Nicholas Ibekwe, released audio that captured Joshua offering cash for friendly stories.) Some reports drew on the judgements of supposed engineers, whose papers had hastily appeared in obscure pay-to-publish journals (one such paper, by Michael Ola Bolaji, contained 170 references, the vast majority of which were links to Emmanuel TV clips on YouTube with titles like 'Face to Face with Lucifer!' and 'Human Possessed by Lizard Demon!').

In 2015, a coroner's inquest ruled that SCOAN was guilty of causing death through criminal negligence. They found that the guesthouse was constructed poorly, using substandard building materials, without planning permission or input from a structural engineer. Builders had added two extra floors to the guesthouse without making changes to the foundations.

Such collapses were not uncommon. In the previous decade, a number of Nigerian schools and residential buildings had collapsed, each killing dozens of people. What made this unusual was not just the number of victims, but the status of SCOAN. It was the biggest tourist attraction in Nigeria. Out of every ten foreign visitors flying into the city, six were heading to the church. If anyone in Nigeria had the funds to build robust buildings, it was TB Joshua. The collapse reflected something fundamental to life at SCOAN: the pursuit of endless growth and greatness, unfettered by regulations or outside expertise.

Joshua was summoned to give evidence at the inquest several times but failed to make an appearance. He kept his head down for a few months, avoiding public appearances and letting disciples take services. Then he returned. A criminal case was brought against SCOAN by the Lagos State government, but the case got nowhere, mired in endless adjournments and delays. The church resumed its status as the number one tourist destination in Nigeria, even while rubble from the guesthouse still lay in the accommodation complex, like the ultimate one-star review.

For a while, Ian kept the blog updated, writing about the inquest, the court case, the South African families attempting to sue. I respected his zeal and persistence, but I didn't share it. The blog had never felt more futile. It was as if Joshua had achieved a state of pure shamelessness that left him bullet-proof, gravity-defying. His identity as Man of God did not need success to sustain it: it could just as well feast on its own failures.

Soon, TB Joshua Watch fell dormant. Meanwhile, 'Watch TB Joshua' – one of the copycat blogs started by SCOAN disciples – was still creating new content every week. Later, we heard from Dan and Kate that two more disciples had left. One was Elliot, the only ex-Immanuel disciple who was not a Winfield. The other was Mary, Dan's sister, who'd appeared in the comments section as Radicalised.

In June 2019, my dad got a friend request from Mary on LinkedIn. He wrote her a short note asking how she was. It would be good to catch up, he said, and invited her to come and visit. My parents had moved out of Winchester about a decade before and lived on the edge of the New Forest. Mary replied with a short message. She was doing OK, readjusting to life outside SCOAN, living in a flat in Basingstoke with her cat. She agreed to visit, and they settled on a date. I wasn't planning to come – she'd reached out to my parents, not me – until Dan and Kate emailed to say that they were also coming. They said that Mary knew about the book and wanted to speak to me.

My wife, daughter and I arrived at the house just before Mary. First there were introductions and small talk over coffee and home-made flapjacks. Mary told us she'd returned to the UK from Lagos at the end of 2017. It had taken several months after that, she said, to really leave SCOAN behind. Since then, she'd been reconnecting with a number of ex-Immanuelites. She'd got an apprenticeship in an IT company in Basingstoke, which had turned into a permanent job. One of the strange things about leaving SCOAN, she said, was how her relationship to time had changed. Disciple life was either endless waiting or relentless, repetitive activity. Except on occasional trips abroad, there was no leisure, no socializing. It felt like more time had passed in the last two years, she said, than in the fourteen years at SCOAN.

What she said accounted for the uncanny feeling of looking at her. She'd moved through time differently to me. It was the same vertiginous feeling I got in my early twenties when I saw an old classmate who'd got pregnant as a teenager, pushing a double buggy through town, looking thoroughly grown-up and worn-out. Here the effect was the opposite. Mary had been held in a kind of stasis of selfhood since the age of seventeen. She looked entirely as she should have – a thirty-something version of the teen I'd once known – but there was something adolescent in her. A newness, tender and unsteady, like that of a fawn finding its legs.

I asked Mary what had made her leave. At first, she said, it was a gradual shift. In 2016, she started working with a small team of outside consultants, who'd come to live at SCOAN while they overhauled the church's outdated IT systems. The consultants were Christians, but they were unaffected by the pressures of disciple life. As they worked alongside Mary, they would ask her questions that seemed shockingly personal, apparently in a spirit of innocent curiosity. 'How long are you guys going to stay here?' 'Are you disciples ever going to get married?' She'd respond in the usual way – 'We need to stay focused on the reasons we're here!', but they were not intimidated in the way that disciples were. They'd challenge her on aspects of church life that made no sense to them. Though she would defend SCOAN in these conversations, their questions lingered on in her mind. After thirteen years at the church, she felt increasingly directionless and unfulfilled. For all the endless toil, she seemed to be getting nowhere.

Then Mary experienced a period of *addaba* unlike any other. She told me she didn't want to speak on the record about the precise reasons for the punishment – the details remained too painful for her – but I recognised the outline of her story only too well. It was not a mistake or misdemeanour that got her in trouble, but a moment of human connection. As with Giles going on a family reunion, or Dan warmly reassuring his mum, her actions provoked Joshua's wrath to the extent that they threatened his absolute power over her self-worth. After being summoned to TB Joshua's office, she emerged in a state of shock, entirely believing his words: that what she'd done was abhorrent, sinful, a sign of demonic possession.

Her remorse was total. Each day she'd get up early in the morning and stand on the gallery – the first-floor seating area overlooking the auditorium that linked the offices and the dorms. She'd stand to the side, averting her eyes from the disciples on errands who walked briskly past. At mealtimes, everyone in the dining room would blank her as she wolfed down her food before going back upstairs. When she knew that TB Joshua was busy in his office, she'd sometimes rest on a chair, but was always vigilant; she had to be standing up when he emerged. She couldn't even be seen reading the Bible or studying her notes, activities that were considered privileges. Over the years, she'd been through many such stretches, sometimes lasting over a fortnight. This time, five weeks passed with no end in sight.

During times when Joshua left the church – as on his regular trips to Prayer Mountain – Mary was not obliged to stay on the gallery, though since she was robbed of all duties, there were few other places she was able to be. She would find a quiet pew in the far end of the church, away from other disciples, where she could read her bible, or just sit and cry.

One day, she decided to be bold. She knew that Joshua sometimes favoured those who took initiative. She waited until after a service, when he tended to be in a good mood. He'd gone upstairs to the Presidential room, the grand dining area in which he usually ate. Church staff had taken in his food. When they went up to retrieve his dishes, she tailed them, slipping into the room. The minute she met his eyes and opened her mouth to ask for forgiveness, she realized she'd made a mistake. He shouted, his eyes

183

wide, lashing his hand towards the door: 'Get out of my face!'

In the days of utter brokenness that followed, she came across a verse in Romans chapter eight that gave her pause. *Therefore, there is now no condemnation for those who are in Christ Jesus.* It occurred to her that God must have forgiven her already. She'd repented, had been so full of remorse that she'd been crying for over a month. Looking back, she realized it was the first time as a disciple that she'd been able to see her relationship with God and TB Joshua as two separate things. If God was forgiving, then TB Joshua was cruel.

The *addaba* lasted around six weeks. Soon after it came to an end, she was sent home, along with several other disciples. Over the next few months, she spent some days yearning to be asked back to the Synagogue Church, and other days beginning to imagine a life beyond it. She stayed with her parents, who were temporarily living in Mexico, then moved in with friends in the UK. She was involved in some foreign trips with SCOAN over the coming months. By February 2018, she'd made up her mind. She sent an email explaining to Joshua that she no longer wanted to be a disciple.

At SCOAN, Mary had always believed that the sexual abuse allegations were lies, in part because she'd never experienced such things herself." In the months after leaving, she talked at length to Kate and Dan. She spoke to a number of other ex-disciples. The accounts she heard did more than just corroborate Kate's story. They backed up Bisola Johnson's allegations of widespread, systematic abuse. Adult disciples were not the only ones Joshua targeted. There were Nigerian girls as young as fourteen, brought up at SCOAN and groomed for sexual exploitation.

When Mary told her parents she was leaving, their response was familiar. 'I think they thought I'd been led astray,' she told me. 'By demons, or Satan, or Dan, or whatever...' Their commitment to SCOAN was unshaken.

Dan and Kate and their two children arrived before dinner. My mum had made a vegetable tagine with chickpeas and apricots. We laid the table in the conservatory and sat down to eat. During dinner, we got talking about TB Joshua Watch. Mary had first found it while working in the email and website department. She would search the internet for any mention of TB Joshua, print out the articles and briefly summarize them to the prophet, who'd ask her to read out the ones that interested him.

She recalled TB Joshua's anger when she first brought the blog to his attention. He blamed Dan and Kate, and when she said she didn't think they were behind it, Joshua accused her of trying to shift the blame away from her family. She brought new posts to read to him a few times, but stopped when she realized that it always got her into trouble. The other sisters would continue to present the latest posts. They would eventually find more effective ways to counter the blog, paying large sums to a reputation management company from the US to help push it from the first page of google results to the wilderness of the fourth or fifth.

Mary would often fall into 'we' when speaking of disciples, and sometimes in the present tense: we do this, we believe that. She caught herself once or twice, and clarified she no longer considered herself one of them. The slippage was entirely understandable, though it was more than just a verbal one. There were flashes of Sister Mary in the room that day. You could feel her fierce loyalty, her hostility to all that was unserious.

There were things, she said, that we got completely wrong on the blog. She mentioned one example: we
shared a news story a few months after the guesthouse
collapse that reported that SCOAN had been desert-
ed by visitors, leaving surrounding businesses in crisis.
This was rubbish, she said. There was no crisis; visitor
numbers remained high. Fair enough, I said, and our
combined instinct for conflict avoidance moved the
conversation on. But I was suddenly conscious of the
blog's irreverent tone, the gleeful abandon with which
we mocked TB Joshua. The blog's mission was sincere
enough, but it was based on the premise that TB Joshua's
ministry was not just abusive, but ridiculous.

The task that faced Mary could not have been more
serious. It was an immense grief, a sifting through rubble. Later Mary would talk about the things she missed
about SCOAN: the sense of purpose and teamwork, the
middle-aged Nigerian women who worked at the SCOAN
grocery store, their friendly banter and maternal tenderness. For fourteen years, SCOAN was everything to her.
Now she was trying to figure out who she was without it.

There was a spare room in my parents' house that was
known as the music room. There was a sofa bed in one
corner, and the other corner was stacked with instruments: a djembe, a cajon, a hang drum, and a collection
of shakers and tin whistles. There was a piano along one
wall, and the old drumkit from Immanuel next to it. My
parents had picked this up after the church disbanded,
along with some folders of sheet music and a couple of
editions of the Mission Praise songbook.

To have dinner at my parents', the Winfields would
discover, was to risk being persuaded into a jam by my
dad. After dinner, a few of us moved into the music room.
Leah and Jake, now nine and five, found percussion

instruments. My daughter, aged one-and-a-half, chose the maracas. I picked up a guitar. Some adults cradled cups of tea and smiled politely. Others found their way to instruments. A joyful noise followed, albeit more joyful for the players than the listeners. Mary didn't play at first, but she softened around the kids, and joined in with the silliness. When the cacophony died down, I asked her if she still played the guitar. She hadn't played since going out to SCOAN, she said. She'd mentioned this predicament over dinner: to rediscover what she enjoyed, she had to go all the way back to her teens. I asked if she could remember anything. She picked up the guitar and sat down. Her fingers found their way into the shape of a D major chord, and she started to fingerpick a gentle, melancholy riff that was faintly familiar to me. I asked her what it was. 'Jars of Clay,' she said. She played it slowly and haltingly at first, and then more fluently: a ringing open chord that repeated and shifted as a thumbed bassline descended.

A few months after we met, I caught up with Mary over videocall. She told me how she'd been focusing on her fitness: she'd recently taken up running. She spoke about her job, about learning to manage the waves of *adda-ba*-like shame that hit her when she made the smallest mistake. She talked about her parents.

She still saw them occasionally, and they communicated regularly by text. 'Whenever they contact me,' she said, 'it messes up my mood. I know it shouldn't, but it does.' When they met up, they made small talk and exchanged news. Her parents were not hostile towards her, but they talked in a polite, superficial tone. There was no heartfelt connection.

Dan and Kate had told me the same. They'd stopped bringing Leah and Jake when they visited them. Dan's parents would always talk about the humanitarian work they were doing through SCOAN – the orphans they were feeding, the difference they'd made. They spoke about how well their other children inside the church were doing. They remained cold and formal towards their grandchildren. 'It's difficult,' Dan told me. 'We've been there ourselves. I feel a little bit angry. But more sad than angry. You're not seeing the real person.'

Dan realized it was so much harder for his parents to leave SCOAN than it had been for him and Kate, who could at least blame the naivety of youth. For the sake of SCOAN, Susan and Gavin had sold property, left behind jobs, and lost relationships with relatives and friends. They'd encouraged their children to forgo education and careers to dedicate their lives to TB Joshua. It struck me that their emotional distance – entirely uncharacteristic of the couple that I knew from Immanuel – masked a silent struggle. To be swayed by affectionate, familial bonds was to show weakness. It was not only that such tenderness towards blasphemers could distract them from their vision. It could cause the whole edifice to collapse.

Mary told me that she had begun to lose her parents in 2002, when she became a disciple. She still saw them back then, but they were friendly and remote: brothers and sisters like the other disciples. At the time she didn't feel the loss, or, at least, was unable to name it. The hurt came out occasionally, in great bursts of emotion that were incomprehensible to her. When she left, she said, all the emotions came to the surface. She suddenly missed her parents terribly. The loss was made harder, she said, by the fact that they were physically present.

She'd decided to have regular contact with them, despite their remoteness. She wanted to be there for them if they decided to leave. 'And I realize,' she said, 'that they could die. They're in their sixties now. I don't want them to die before knowing the truth. And not just knowing the truth, but actually healing from it. That takes time.'

Before the end of my call with Mary, we spoke about the day at my parents' place. I asked Mary the name of the Jars of Clay song that she played on guitar. She said it was 'Frail', a song from the album *Much Afraid*. I listened to the song on YouTube later, and immediately recognized it: the fingerpicked riff, the echoing snare drum, the sweet dissonance of the string section that climbed and climbed then resolved into harmony.

Revisiting Christian music from my past meant re-awakening the teenager in me who once loved it, without silencing the adult music snob of the present. Often the adult won out. Sometimes, as with the grungy rap-rock of 'Jesus Freak' by DC Talk, the two selves would reach a deadlock and the song would remain simultaneously awesome and terrible. The song 'Frail' was one I knew well, but I never owned the album; Jars of Clay were a bit adult-contemporary for the teenage me. Listening to it now, it moved me more than it ever did when I was younger. Had I ever paid attention to the lyrics before? The words were tender, meditative and uncertain; a world apart from the Jesus-pushing of other Christian bands. 'If I was not so weak,' went the chorus, 'if I was not so cold, if I was not so scared of being broken, growing old, I would be frail.'

The wording was strange and circular, but I recognized the paradox – 'for when I am weak, then I am strong' – from Paul's letter to the Corinthians. This idea was not entirely alien to the revivalist worldview. 'For the sake of Christ, then,' wrote Paul in the same letter, 'I am content with weaknesses, insults, hardships, persecutions, and calamities.' The likes of Tommy Tenney sold broken-ness and self-flagellation as a means to an end. It was a phase to pass through, white-knuckled, on the way to some imagined breakthrough: revival, baptism in the spirit, Christian perfection. TB Joshua had a genius for exploiting this feature; SCOAN disciples took their un-happy and embattled state as a sign they were on the path of righteousness. The song proposed something entire-ly different to the revivalist's pursuit of certainty. We're condemned to a state of great weakness, it suggested, if we don't accept our frailty, our individual finitude, our propensity to mess things up.

I don't know exactly when I first heard 'Frail'. It was almost certainly at the Winfields' house in around 1997, probably on a Sunday afternoon. There was often a crowd there for Sunday lunch. After we finished the meal, the adults would hang out in the kitchen and dining room. My siblings and I, along with any other Immanuel youth, would head with Dan and his brother and sisters into the living room.

There was a large, comfortable three-piece suite, a thick carpet, tasteful art prints on the wall, a hi-fi and a TV in the corner. We'd sit around and watch videos from the Winfields' Christian music collection. Some were compilation videos from US record labels, others were video albums or full-length concerts. We'd watch Jars of Clay, their floppy fringes and baggy shirts and mandolins. We'd watch DC Talk live in concert: the speaker stacks, the dancers, the pogoing crowds. We'd watch Carman, the sharp-suited, middle-aged crooner-turned-rapper, who had the biggest special effects budget in all contem-porary Christian music. In one video, he plays a Christian gunslinger, walking into a Western saloon full of latex devils, to a soundtrack that was part-'Thriller', part-

Fistful of Dollars. He slays demons one by one, sending them sprawling around the bar: Alcoholism, Infirmity, False Religion. Then he faces his final adversary and unloads his anointed six-shooter at point-blank range: 'Satan...' he says. 'Bite the dust!'

When I watched the video now, I couldn't help thinking of the exorcisms at SCOAN: the death throes of the Spirit of Death, the Spirit of Lust. I also remembered that living room, those friends, our shared gaze at the glowing screen. We sat together and drank it all in: the good songs and the bad songs, the wisdom and the folly, the visions and the demons and the ordinary grace.

V. VISIONS

On my second day in Lagos, I went to a Christian bookshop in Ikoyi. The shop, like many businesses in this affluent area of Lagos, had a high metal gate, bars on the windows, and a security guard stationed outside. It was not exclusively religious – there was also a selection of secular novels and non-fiction – but as I walked in, the shelves radiated the visual language of Christian publishing. The trees and sunrises of the inspirational titles: *Empowered from Above, Positioned to Bless*. The fiery reds and blacks of the apocalyptic: *Four Blood Moons, Jerusalem Countdown*. There was a section for Nigerian authors, but most of the shop floor was taken up by Americans and Brits, along with a few global evangelical megastars like the South Korean Paul Yonggi Cho. I quickly found the big names from Immanuel's revival days – Tommy Tenney, Rick Joyner, Smith Wigglesworth, Watchman Nee.

I was drawn to a large rotating display near the till, which held dozens of pamphlets, mostly by American evangelists. They were small, cheap, stapled booklets, some faintly yellowed with age. I flicked through one by Kenneth Hagin, and another by Billie Joe Daugherty, both printed in Tulsa, Oklahoma, and first published in the 1980s. They were written in a simple, folksy American English. 'I talk to the Lord like I talk to you,' wrote Kenneth Hagin in *What God Taught Me About Prosperity*, 'because he knows what we sound like anyway; there's no use in our putting on airs.' These pamphlets seemed out of place in the air-conditioned stillness of this upmarket bookshop, surrounded by the glossy $20 paperbacks on the main shelves. Their natural habitat might have been a bookstall in a Lagos marketplace, or the table at the back of a revival meeting, or the right hand of a commuter in a packed *danfo* minibus. I took a handful of tracts to the till to pay for them, then headed out to join Pastor Isaac, who was waiting for me in the car.

On the drive to the bookshop, we'd passed a church every hundred metres or so. Some were opulent, all marble and classical pillars, others large and warehouse-like, and others more modest, like small-town business centres. I'd jotted down names as they went by. For all the variety of the buildings, the names formed a verbal skyline of towering righteousness: The Lord's Scepter, Seed of David, Foundation of Truth Assembly, Divine Appointments Ministry.

Lagos was a city saturated with Pentecostal churches. It hadn't always been like this. In the late '80s and early '90s, Nigerian pastors had shared prophecies that were almost identical to those we heard in Immanuel. 'Nigeria is indeed poised for a revival of an unprecedented dimension,' wrote Pastor M. O. Ojewale in 1990. 'The early showers ... have begun already.' The difference was that in Nigeria the vision, or something not unlike it, had come to pass. These imported ideas – the everyday demonology, the triumphalist End Times vision, the God whose gifts of health, wealth and power were simply waiting to be claimed – had spread through the urban centres of Nigeria with a rapidity and reach unprecedented in the Western countries from which they'd originated.

As we drove through the city, the pamphlets felt vaguely talismanic in my hands. As flimsy and unassuming as they were, they were vessels for ideas that had transformed millions of lives. I wondered when TB Joshua had first read such pamphlets, and glimpsed a future in the vision they evoked.

193

I didn't go to Lagos to visit SCOAN. I was still confounded by the extent of Joshua's power and influence, the persistence of his success after the catastrophe of the guesthouse collapse. But I doubted that attending a service would have given me any more insight. I'd already watched a lifetime's worth of Emmanuel TV. Instead, I wanted a sense of the context out of which Joshua had emerged.

Or that was what I'd told myself. There were other reasons for directing my focus elsewhere. Before I left, my wife had made me promise that I wouldn't visit the Synagogue Church. I hadn't taken too much persuasion. Although I'd written the blog anonymously, I knew that the Immanuelite disciples would have recognized me and immediately known my critical intent. Not all the scenarios that had run through my head were dangerous, but they were all awkward. My six days in Lagos, I decided, would be a chance to see the city, visit other megachurches, immerse myself in Nigerian Pentecostalism, the wider movement in which TB Joshua, for all his global fame, was only a footnote.

Of course, from the moment I arrived in Murtala Muhammed airport, SCOAN was on my mind. As I waited at the conveyor belt for the baggage to arrive, I imagined Pastor Graham pacing this same hall, his body stiff with pain. As I was driven down the main road, I watched *okadas* passing in the opposite lane and thought of Dan and Kate. The next morning, I woke up in the thick Lagos heat to the sound of a ringtone. When I picked up the buzzing mobile beside my bed, I was startled to see 'Daddy' on the caller ID. It took me a moment to realize that the phone, lent to me by my host Desmond since I lacked a local SIM card, had been last used by his daughter.

194

Throughout the week, I asked a number of people I came across – largely Christians, unaffiliated with the Synagogue Church – what they thought of TB Joshua. People gave various answers, but they all shared a reticence to talk. Some laughed warily. Others said they'd heard some good things about him, and some bad things, and they weren't in a place to judge. Others clearly had lots to say, but kept a cautious silence. One man, who asked to remain anonymous, shook his head when I asked the question. 'When Satan fell from heaven,' he said, 'he landed in Nigeria. There is too much juju here!'

I was familiar with this line of criticism. Bisola Johnson had alleged that she'd witnessed many occult activities at SCOAN: bizarre rituals, animal sacrifice, and TB Joshua's notes, written in a mysterious script, that he handed to people with the intention of influencing their dreams. Between Joshua's most vehement Nigerian critics, and his most ardent Western supporters, here was one shared conviction: that the most salient fact about him was his supposedly unrefined 'African-ness'. His critics said his Christianity was skin-deep – scratch the surface, and you'd find a *babalawo*, or witch doctor. For Western supporters like the Winfields, his lack of exposure to Western culture and education made him a purer vessel for the gifts of the spirit.

The former claim was more plausible than the latter. Across West Africa, the Americas and the Caribbean, the worship of traditional Yoruban deities known as *orisha* has proved remarkably adaptive and persistent, surviving conversion to Christianity and the violent dislocations of the slave trade. It was not unlikely that there were pre-Christian influences on the Synagogue Church – Joshua had started his religious life as a junior prophet at the Celestial Christian Church of God, a group well

195

known for its syncretic rituals – but he was more a product of the West than most of his critics and supporters would suggest.

In the early years of the blog, Dan Winfield had sent us a large cache of Quotable Quotes in the form of a Word document. These were the supposedly sacred words of TB Joshua that Dan had spent long hours transcribing and memorising as a young disciple, convinced that their uncanny, fragmented eloquence was proof that Joshua was channelling something beyond himself. It turned out that this was true. We put the document through an academic plagiarism detector, and found that around 19 per cent of the text was plagiarized, lifted directly from US evangelists like Billy Joe Daugherty and Don De Welt.

Some of Joshua's influences were overt. On the walls of the Synagogue Church, there were framed pictures of famous, predominantly American evangelists: a group dubbed God's Generals by the US writer Roberts Liairdon in his book of the same name. Disciples told me that Joshua often spoke of this book. Kate Winfield gave me her copy, originally a gift from him, complete with a personal transcription. The book is a 'how to' guide for aspiring revivalists, drawing lessons from the life stories of the generals. 'You CAN gain the victory in your life and ministry,' proclaimed the back cover. 'Let God's Generals show you how!' The 'generals' were a varied bunch. There was Aimee Semple McPherson, whose LA megachurch, known for its theatricality and claims of healing, attracted both the masses and the Hollywood elite. There was Charles Parham, born in 1873, a Ku Klux Klan-sympathizing Bible teacher from Topeka, Kansas, and his former student William J Seymour, the African American son of former slaves. Seymour, who had to listen to Parham's lectures from the corridor due to segregation laws, went on to lead the Asuza Street Mission, the exuberant multiracial church in Los Angeles that became the epicentre of modern Pentecostalism, attracting visitors from around the US and prompting evangelical missions to China, India and Africa.

The lives of these evangelists exemplified, at least in Liairdon's telling, the man or woman of God as entrepreneur: driven, individualist and charismatic, contemptuous of the checks and balances of the law or denominational church. Several touched on a trope that TB Joshua's own story leaned heavily on: that of the unlettered Man of God. He was clearly literate enough to have gathered – perhaps from Liairdon's stories of Smith Wigglesworth and William Branham – that his lack of formal education could be invoked to authenticate his prophetic gifts.

The stories in God's Generals tended to be faith-boosting anecdotes rather than rigorous historical accounts, but they were not uncritical hagiographies. The book lived up to its subtitle: 'How They Succeeded, and How Some Failed'. The lives of several of the 'generals' ended in disillusion or disgrace. John Alexander Dowey ended up a figure of ridicule after declaring himself to be the reincarnation of the Prophet Elijah and founding his own city (Zion, Illinois) in preparation for the Second Coming. AA Allen, famed for his healing ministry, drank himself to death in a Californian hotel room. The lessons Liairdon draws from these stories are vague and impractical. Mistakes happen, he suggests, when people follow the ego or the suggestions of others over God's call – as if distinguishing between these competing voices was a straightforward thing. It's notable that the qualities to which Liairdon attributes the successes of the generals – the limitless faith in the greatness of their destiny, the disregard for criticism or constraint – were often instrumental in their equally dramatic fall.

Joshua had found his vocation as Man of God in a time of crisis in Nigeria. After the high oil prices of the early 70s prompted a decade of state spending and dramatic growth, their subsequent fall left Nigeria on the edge of an economic precipice. By 1986, the military regime was forced by the International Monetary Fund to accept a structural adjustment plan to facilitate the repayment of debts. The currency was radically devalued. State services collapsed. Much of the emergent middle class was plunged into poverty. There was a wave of violent crime: kidnappings, car-jackings, home invasions. Meanwhile, a well-connected elite made a fortune from the opening up of the economy. It was in this era that a new form of American Pentecostal Christianity took hold in Nigeria, arriving through radio broadcasts, visiting preachers, and books and pamphlets shipped across the Atlantic from the American Bible Belt. To talk of Pentecostalism in the West is to talk of churches with a specific lineage, traced back to the Asuza Street revival in 1906. The Pentecostal boom in West Africa has blurred the sectarian boundaries. The term describes a cultural shift across and beyond denomination, towards a fervent modern style of worship, a belief in the gifts of the spirit, and a worldview revolving around the twin poles of apocalyptic revivalism and Dale Carnegie-style self-improvement.

There are scholars that argue that this rise in Pentecostal Christianity in Nigeria amounted to a kind of neo-imperialism. At a time when Western financial institutions were imposing brutal austerity measures, Western evangelists came to Nigeria preaching a prosperity gospel which taught people they could pray their way out of poverty, and that the struggle which mattered was in the spiritual realm, not the political. Other scholars, like the Nigerian theologian Ogbu Kalu, pay more attention to the ways in which Nigerians have taken this way of doing church and made it serve their own needs.

'The holy spirit has diverse operations!' said Pastor Isaac. He was driving me from the bookshop in Ikoyi to a shopping mall in Lekki where he'd suggested we get dinner. 'There are churches,' he said, 'who have a gift for healing. There are other ministries whose whole gift is for babies. Couples who are barren are prayed for, and they are able to conceive. There are some churches whose pastor has a gift for messages of hope and restoration. You can't beat them at it! When they open their mouth to preach, the person who has already planned to commit suicide will have a change of heart!'

Isaac was in his early forties but looked younger. He wore a crisp pinstriped shirt with cuff-links. At times he'd speak reflectively, pausing to consider his answers. Other times he'd fall into well-worn grooves of teaching and testimony, as the steering wheel became a pulpit and I a reluctant one-man congregation, munching on street-vendor peanuts in the passenger seat. Once he stopped himself, laughed, and apologized for going into preacher mode. Waiting at a red light on Victoria Island, he spotted an old friend queuing in the adjacent lane. He smiled and wound the window down. 'Behave yourself!' he shouted to him, jabbing a finger in mock admonition. 'I am watching you!'

We passed, from a distance, the elegant white monolith of the House on the Rock, the church in which Isaac served as a junior pastor. Led by Pastor Paul Adefarasin, an architect by background, the church catered to a largely young professional, cosmopolitan crowd. I'd attend a Sunday service there later in my visit. On the walls of its sleek foyer, framed portraits displayed an idiosyncratic lineage, ending with Pastor Paul. There was Samuel Ajayi Crowther, Nigeria's first Anglican bishop, Julius Nyerere, the Pan African leftist leader, and the arch-capitalist Henry Ford.

Isaac told me that he'd first attended a service at the House on the Rock twelve years ago. He was a backslidden Christian in his early twenties, struggling with depression and drug addiction. In his sermon, Pastor Paul spoke about his own youthful battle with addiction. At once, Isaac recognized his own lostness, and glimpsed a vision of a different future. He re-committed his life to Christ that day. It was the first step, he told me, that led him to train to become a pastor himself.

One church we passed was huge and derelict. Its besuited pastor stared out confidently from a canvas banner that was starting to sag. Its mirrored glass was still shining, but half of the windows were broken, exposing burned interiors, torn upholstery, and what looked like squatters' laundry, hanging out to dry.

Some pastors reached great heights of fame and wealth, Isaac explained, and then disappeared. 'They were misled by the prosperity message. They are now in the shadows. No-one knows what they are doing. I see them as fraudsters. There was a famous pastor who said, "God does not hear the prayer of a poor man!"' He slapped the steering wheel. 'Ah! Can you imagine? The prayer of the poor is not heard!? Then who is God hearing? You see how some have abused the gospel?'

Isaac explained that the pastor was trying to raise an offering, suggesting that only the prayers of generous givers would be answered. It was this kind of thing, he said, that made the Protestants break away from Rome. But these were not the ministries that thrived, he said. It was desperation that pushed people to double down on the prosperity message. A sign that the ministry had a poor foundation, and had entered the phase which preceded collapse.

Pastor Isaac had gained his BA in Theology from Redeemer's University, run by the Redeemed Christian Church of God. The RCCG, one of the largest ministries in Nigeria, straddled two eras of Nigerian Pentecostalism. In the 1970s, Pentecostal Christians, then a small sliver of Nigeria's Christian population, were known for their austerity: drab clothes, second-hand cars, the rejection of the material comforts of the world in favour of holiness. Amid the imposed austerity of the 1980s, it's not hard to see how the 'name it and claim it' teaching preached by the likes of Kenneth Hagin outsold this doctrine of voluntary self-denial. It was a teaching that could appeal to rich and poor alike, offering hope to the have-nots, and reassurance to the wealthy that God bestows riches on the righteous. Pastor E. A. Adeboye, the general overseer of the RCCG since 1980, embraced the belief that being a good Christian was compatible with affluence and material comfort.

'The RCCG does not preach prosperity,' said Pastor Isaac. 'They preach righteousness, holiness. If you do the right things, God will reward you. Money and prosperity is the by-product of living right. If you work hard, if you are diligent, if you build value, what will happen? There will be a reward!'

We passed one or two mosques on our drive, occasional reminders that Christianity was not the only monotheism in town. An estimated 48 per cent of Nigerians are Muslims. Even in this south-western corner of the country, up to 40 per cent of the dominant Yoruba-speaking population are followers of Islam. Many extended families contain Muslims, Christians and followers of traditional religion, whose differences are often superseded by a shared Yoruba identity. The wave of born-again Christianity had impacted the Muslims of Yorubaland in surprising ways.

On my journey into Lagos from the airport, I'd passed a prayer centre belonging to NASFAT, an organization whose full name is Nasrul-Lahi-il-Fathi Society of Nigeria, the pioneers of a fast-growing movement often referred to as 'pentecostal Islam'. NASFAT was founded in 1995 by a group of Yoruba Muslim professionals concerned at the increasing dominance of a new, dynamic Pentecostal Christianity. Their answer was to form a 'pacesetting Islamic organization' that would stem the flow of young Muslims leaving the faith and assert a confident and modern Islamic identity. While promoting a tolerant take on Islamic piety, the leaders of NASFAT also drew explicitly on the elements of Pentecostalism that had been so attractive to Nigerians.

NASFAT targeted the professional class and those aspiring towards it, founding a university, running networking groups, and offering management courses presenting the Prophet Muhammed as an exemplary businessman. The movement encouraged the participation of women, some of whom ascended to leadership roles. NASFAT-linked singers released upbeat songs invoking God and Muhammed, closer in style to gospel music than the austere sonorities of qur'anic recitation. The organization held all-night prayer meetings and sold booklets containing 'prayer points' which promised protection from evil spirits. The principal weekly gathering of the faithful took place not on a Friday but a Sunday, to guard against the twin temptations of idleness and exuberant Christianity. The gathering was known as *asalatu*, from the Arabic for 'prayer', but here, too, some believers took their cue from their Pentecostal brothers and sisters, referring to the meeting as a 'prayer crusade'.

What set TB Joshua apart in this ecosystem? His claimed gifts of prophecy and healing were far from unique. The Synagogue Church had not been able to self-replicate and multiply like the RCCG had. There had been several international branches of SCOAN in the past, but nearly all had shut down. It was a one-man show: TB Joshua had little appetite for delegation, or empowering leaders besides himself.

Perhaps his power was in his freedom from constraint. His outcast status on the Pentecostal scene meant that there were no limits to the outrageousness of his claims. Joshua was able to take the American ideal of the entrepreneurial Man of God to its ultimate expression, far beyond what was possible in the West. In Nigeria, the atrophy of the state and impoverishment of the people meant Joshua was also free from the strictures of public scrutiny or legal accountability. In Lagos, lawyers, journalists and other professionals in full employment would sometimes go for months without a salary. Bribes were not just an indulgence, accepted by the most corrupt. For many they were a lifeline, without which rent or school fees might be impossible to pay.

He was not the only pastor to enjoy this kind of clout. What made him unique, perhaps, was his instinct for a central, albeit implicit, feature of revivalist Christianity. TB Joshua knew how to exploit the power of elsewhereness, the sense that greatness was just beyond the horizon, both temporal – as in his slogan 'the best is yet to come'

– and physical. 'Distance is not a barrier,' he proclaimed on Emmanuel TV, and this was only half the story. Many pastors built their brands by adopting the flashy consumerism and salesman's confidence of American evangelists: the promise of Western prosperity manifesting in local form. It took a trickster genius like Joshua to take the raw materials of Western Christianity and transform them into something to sell back to the West.

Nigerians often lament the way in which their country's abundance of natural resources has failed to translate into lasting prosperity: how they export cheap raw materials like petroleum and palm oil, only to buy them back from abroad in expensive refined form. Far from refining western Pentecostalism, Joshua distressed it, like stonewashed denim, taking advantage of western Christians' yearning for authenticity, and the blind spots of their exoticizing gaze. In turn, the white faces and BBC voices of these disciples – always featured prominently on Emmanuel TV – gave his ministry extra prestige among his Lagos followers, and the attenders of his stadium tours across the global south.

As he dropped me off, Pastor Isaac asked if there was anything else I wanted to see in Lagos: he was free the following day. His offer took me by surprise. I'd also found myself with unexpected free time, having realized the gathering at the RCCG I'd come to attend was starting two days later than I'd thought. 'Could we go to SCOAN?' I asked. 'Sure,' he said.

To get from Lekki in the east of the city to Ikotun-Egbe in the west, it was a four-hour journey. This time, we got a lift with Joseph, who worked as a driver for my host. Heading down Lekki highway, we passed malls, fast-food restaurants, and the grand entrances of gated communities. We passed puddle-pitted ground where traders operated out of wooden huts, their wares piled high beside them: metal rebar, bamboo for scaffolding, large metal gates topped with sharp spikes. We hit go-slows around bridges and intersections, where groups of beggars – large-eyed women and children from whom I'd already learned to avert my gaze – would crowd the car and tap on the windows imploringly. We drove across the bridges that connected Lekki to the high-rise offices of Ikoyi, then launched out across the water towards the Lagos Mainland.

This last bridge – known as the Third Mainland Bridge – was a marvel of engineering. First commissioned in 1976, it was 11.8 kilometres long, arcing across the lagoon like the spine of a giant sea-serpent. A relic of an era of big-state infrastructure projects, it also bore witness – with its crumbling concrete pillars and pot-holed surfaces – to years of subsequent neglect, and the untrammelled growth of the city around it. As we approached the mainland, we could see, to the left of the bridge, the settlement known as Makoko. A dark mass of huts on stilts spread out across the water, a gauze of white smoke hanging overhead. Straining to look closer, I saw the leaning wooden structures, the roofs of corrugated iron and black plastic sheeting, the distant figures on reed canoes.

Makoko was sometimes referred to as a floating slum, and other times as the 'Venice of Africa'. Neither description seemed right. One defined it by its squalor, obscuring the ingenuity of its construction. The other belied the fragility of its status. In 2012, residents were given 72 hours' notice before 3,000 homes were demolished by the government. Makoko, which existed as a fishing community as far back as the 1800s, had in recent decades become home to large numbers of internally displaced people. Many of those left homeless by the demolitions were Ijaw people from the oil-rich Bayelsa state, where their traditional riverine way of life had been disrupted by armed conflict and pollution. The government, perhaps embarrassed by Makoko's proximity to the offices of multinational companies in Ikoyi, had proclaimed that it was an illegal and unsanitary settlement which undermined the 'megacity status' of Lagos. Despite the threat of demolition, Makoko had continued to expand.

The bridge reached the mainland. We drove down broad highways spanned by pedestrian bridges, before turning on to congested streets crowded in with street vendors, lined with rubbish-strewn ditches. Re-joining a main road, we hit a traffic jam so stubborn that several cars around us went back the way they came, bumping over the raised intersection and turning into the incoming traffic. Pastor Isaac had fashioned a kind of couch on the backseat, reclining against his rucksack with his legs stretched out, and scrolling down his phone. Half an hour later we passed the cause of the jam. At a junction, a truck had spilled its load of rocks in the middle of the road. A group of men appeared to be directing traffic around the blockage, though the chaos and shouting suggested a perpetual altercation through which traffic was obliged to pass.

Soon after, we arrived in Ikotun-Egbe. When the synagogue church first came into view, I was struck by its strangeness. Minutes later, I'd see the SCOAN I knew from photos: the Christian kitsch of the giant Bible and the Jesus statue, the row of palm trees. From the front, the church was iconic, a symbol divorced from its surroundings. On the approach, it seemed to emerge organically from the urban sprawl around it.

Along the side of the road, there was a fence of battered corrugated iron sheets covered with a palimpsest of torn adverts: 'Daily job at Juice Company – N3500 per day'; 'Milk company needs workers – N25,000'. The fence rested on a tall wall of grey-brown breezeblock. Thrusting upwards behind this, in the same tannery colours of street level, was the tower of the Synagogue Church. Its tall, broad front was implausibly thin from the side, with a teetering asymmetry – irregular windows, jutting balconies – that suggested a game of Jenga well underway. The textured plaster façade was an inscrutable tangle of intersecting lines. I'd spent years attempting to understand this place. Faced with the building, I felt newly mystified. It was as if in this side view, the true unlikeliness of the church was revealed.

The marvel was not that it stood *despite* its poor foundations. It was not like the houses of Makoko, balanced over the waters of the lagoon against all odds. In the gap between TB Joshua's claimed anointing and its absence, a great energy circulated. The ministry stood like the sides of a whirlpool stood. It was a temple of pure momentum, fuelled by an unending supply of hope, feeding an equally vast runoff of private misery. That of the disciple, wrestling with shame and inadequacy as she pursues an elusive breakthrough. The international pilgrim, escorted out by staff for being too sick for the prayer line. The recipient of prayer, declared healed, whose symptoms are transformed from mortal pain to the bitter fruit of their own doubt.

'Turn right onto Segun Irefin street,' said the American-accented satnav lady, who all morning had been gamely pronouncing Nigerian place names. We turned right, passing the armed police in their hut, the row of flags, the main entrance. As we drove slowly over speed bumps, I looked across the street and saw, through the open gates of the accommodation complex, a pile of rubble: the last remains of the guesthouse, still uncleared after four years. I held up my phone to take a photo of it, then put it down as a security guard walked towards us, waving his hand forbiddingly, and the satnav lady spoke up once again: 'You have reached your destination.'

¶ The folder named 'LAGOS TRIP' lay unvisited on my laptop for a year and a half. There were good reasons for its neglect: work, fatherhood, the writing and re-writing of other chapters. But it was more than a lack of time that kept me away. The contents – many hours of interviews, hundreds of blurry photos, pages of notes and reflections – were at once too much and not enough. I regretted the shortness of my stay, my timid avoidance of SCOAN (we'd turned around and left the minute we arrived, and headed for a lunch of jollof rice), and my hubris in opting for a brief visit to the RCCG instead, a phenomenon that itself could provide the material for several books.

I'd gone to Lagos hoping to make sense of the extraordinary boom in Pentecostal Christianity of which TB Joshua formed a part. What were these megachurches really about, these collectives that had emerged out of conditions of crisis and collapse? Was Joshua's abusive egomania the norm? Were megachurches merely vehicles for individual self-enrichment? Or were some self-sustaining communities, truly corporate rather than just capitalist? Such was the gap between the breadth of my questions and the meagreness of my materials that any attempt to get started seemed to fail. I couldn't listen to more than a few seconds of the recordings without jolts of shame: at the good questions I didn't ask, the ten-minute blocks of sermonizing I didn't interrupt, and my habit of expounding my own opinions at length, as if my purpose of going to Lagos was to tell a handful of Nigerians what I thought about things.

Two months into the first COVID lockdown, I loaded the files onto my mp3 recorder. After dinner, and L's bedtime routine, and the work admin that couldn't wait, I'd grab the recorder and headphones, put on my shoes, and leave the house. I found that as long as my legs were moving, I could settle into the recordings, re-inhabit the conversations, reflect on the interesting bits.

We'd been staying at my parents' place in Fawley since the beginning of lockdown, an escape from the cramped one-bedroom flat in the centre of Southampton that we'd been meaning to leave since L was born. On those night walks, I'd wander down old country roads without street-lights, past hedgerows and towering bramble bushes, under canopies of gnarled oak. I'd walk past illuminated bungalows, dark privet hedges neatly trimmed, magnolia blossoms pale in the moonlight. These were the kind of streets in which the houses had names instead of num-bers: Sea Breeze, Fourfields, Ocean View.

While I walked, I listened to Isaac as he told me about the night in his twenties when he'd first had a vision of becoming a pastor. He'd dreamed that he was standing with Pastor Paul on a stage in front of a huge crowd. His friends laughed at him when he told them the next day. But he felt as if he'd glimpsed something that had already happened, like God had let him step for a moment out-side of linear time. As I walked, the Lagos traffic roared and honked in my ears. Tupac's 'Changes' played on the radio – the soundtrack, Isaac told me, of his wayward youth.

I walked down the long grass verge of the main road, an empty bus throwing long shadows as it passed on the way to Calshot. I walked past the corner shop and empty pub of the village square. Beyond the village, the whole northern sky was lit up orange with gas flares. The oil refinery, owned by ExxonMobil, was the largest in the country, and the main employer in the area. The village was nestled against its southern perimeter, like a small suburb on the edge of a sprawling metropolis.

The industrial skyline here was so familiar to me that

its presence was almost homely. Both my grandmothers lived nearby. Every other weekend in my childhood, I'd gaze at the refinery sleepily from the backseat of the car on the way back to Winchester: the tall cylindrical towers, the huge squat storage tanks mottled with rust, the vast complexity of pipes, ladders and walkways. The gas flares were a kind of safety valve, burning off the excess gas produced when crude oil was heated and broken down into its constituent parts. On these quiet summer nights, with looming catastrophes in the news, the knowledge that these flames were routine did not dispel the unease they provoked. The horizon was on fire. It was hard not to see the situation for what it was.

'A vision,' Pastor Isaac said, 'is like a laser. It concentrates many rays of light into a single beam. If you place a piece of paper under it, what does it do? The laser penetrates it! That's what a vision does. When you are focused, when you have all your energies channelled together, you penetrate, you break through barriers, you become who God told you to be.'

It had been the right decision to come to Fawley. We were lucky to have had the option. It was a bit cramped, the three of us sharing an upstairs spare room, but L loved the grandparents and the garden. I worked three days a week, took L for one, and wrote on another. My mum had offered to help out with childcare so that M and I could continue our respective projects alongside work: my book, M's part-time degree. The pandemic seemed to have drawn out some atavistic instinct in me: an urge to hunker down with the wider family and weather the storm together. On a good day, at least, this seemed a persuasive story, but there were less flattering interpretations. Other days, our predicament reminded me of everything we didn't have as a family of three.

I'd been writing this book for nearly five years now. For at least two, I'd been convinced that it was nearly done. I'd been putting off working full-time, learning to drive, and moving to a bigger place until it was over. I'd been neglecting exercise, hobbies, relationships, in my pursuit of this vision perpetually just over the horizon. And now my wife was stuck with her in-laws, and we'd missed our chance to get on the property ladder before the apocalypse.

My therapy work had moved online. In the weeks after the pandemic hit, colleagues had forwarded email after email by therapists and experts containing bullet-pointed hints and tips for promoting resilience, managing Covid-anxiety, adapting therapy to the conditions of a pandemic. Like dogs barking and toads leaping from ponds before an earthquake hits, when faced with the radical uncertainty of a pandemic, CBT therapists wrote tip sheets. We'd do the same, I imagined, if an asteroid was hurtling towards earth. *Try limiting your news intake to 5 minutes a day. Take exercize if you can. Remember to check in with colleagues: a small word, a little help, can make a big difference.*

In many of my one-to-one sessions, I felt oddly redundant. My caseload – people who'd sought help for anxiety or depression in the Before Times – now seemed like a random sample of the population. For some, lockdown had been a relief, a welcome chance to reconnect or recuperate. For others, the pandemic had left them stuck in a way that lockdown made near impossible to change. Somewhere out there, there were surely legions of the newly anxious or depressed, but they hadn't reached us yet. Sessions often felt as if the parts of therapist and patient had been assigned arbitrarily, as in a roleplay. It seemed absurd that I should know any better than anyone else how to live in these times. I gathered the obligatory questionnaire scores, but they felt less meaningful than usual. Surely all standards of healthy normality needed to be suspended until further notice. I wondered if the conditions necessary for this fiction would ever return.

It was in therapy groups that I felt most purposeful. With a colleague, I ran a group called 'Comprehend, Cope and Connect', a third-wave CBT programme for people who struggled with intense emotions, who often had backgrounds of childhood adversity or trauma. The programme didn't work for everyone, and at the end of each course, the members scattered to the wind. But when a group was going well, it became a kind of living organism within which otherwise unnameable truths could be named, and the self could be seen in a new light, held with an unfamiliar kindness. It was a happy surprise that at least some of the dynamics of the group appeared to survive the transition to screen.

Maybe these groups moved me because they fostered, among the participants, a connectedness that was missing in my own life. Or perhaps what I liked best was what the group drew from me. I was a good facilitator. Outside the group, I had never been less focused, less equanimous. I was as brain-fogged and lethargic and anxious as I'd ever been. But I liked who I was when I was leading a discussion with the group, deploying a good metaphor, doing a mindfulness exercise. Notice your weight in the chair. Notice your spine holding up your body, your head on top of your spine. Notice any thoughts or judgements as they arise, and gently let them go.

Perhaps this was partly why I liked Pastor Isaac, and why, as I listened back to our conversations, he both charmed and frustrated me. He spoke well, and in his passionate sermonizing, I recognized my own love of coherence-seeking, articulating, inspiring an audience. I knew that this compulsive sense-making could sometimes be a substitute for wisdom rather than its expression. It could be a kind of skating over ice, the sheer velocity keeping you upright, keeping the cracks from spreading and the water from swallowing you up. Yet maybe he had something I lacked.

I liked that image of a laser. I was surprised by its pragmatism: the suggestion that a divine vision did not promise access to miracles or divine favour, but allowed you to focus and channel your diffuse human energies, helping you achieve the otherwise unachievable. The best thinkers of Western psychology could offer valuable tools for psychological flexibility: ways of unhooking from unhelpful stories and returning to the present, ways of shifting how we related to ourselves and our emotions. When it came to finding a vision – one that focused, galvanized, bound us to others – we were on our own.

Isaac had built a life around this vision, in a place in which the most basic errands demanded a fortitude that was alien to me. And it seemed to be working for him. When we had lunch in a café in Lekki, Isaac showed me a photo on his phone. It was taken ten years after he'd first been called to ministry, when he'd started working as a junior pastor in the House on the Rock. He stood with Pastor Paul before a vast crowd, in the huge outdoor gospel event known as The Experience. After years of study and apprenticeship, his dream had come to pass.

At one point, driving in the car, Isaac's voice lowered almost to a whisper. 'These are horrible times for Nigeria,' he said. Just in the last week, a hundred soldiers were killed by Boko Haram in a single attack in the north-east of the country. And the violence was moving south. In the

214

Middle Belt, armed Fulani herders had been escalating attacks on mostly Christian farmers, killing hundreds, forcing hundreds of thousands to flee their homes. In one attack, he said, a pregnant women was slaughtered, and her unborn baby was torn from her womb. Until recently, he said, Christian leaders emphasized prayer over political action. Now this was changing.

'About ten years ago, it dawned on E. A. Adeboye that if we do not take part in politics or governance, in nation building, then we are going to lose this nation, probably to a genocidal war. Because we are allowing the wrong people to occupy that space. Now when light does not occupy a space, what comes in is darkness – am I right? Because darkness has always occupied that space, when light begins to shine, what do you expect? Resistance! So that's the resistance that we've been experiencing with all the bombings, the killings, the persecutions.'

'What do you mean by darkness?' I asked.

'I mean corruption, Islamization,' he said. 'All the negative things that happen when you put the wrong people in positions of governance.'

Listening back, I could hear the discomfort in my voice, my instinctive unease with this sectarian view of Nigerian politics only matched by my own ignorance of the terrible topic at hand. 'Isn't the cure for Islamization a stronger secular national identity?' I asked. 'If you are meeting Islamization with Christianization, isn't the conflict going to deepen?'

After my trip, I read more about the violence in the Middle Belt. The Fulani herders were nomads from the North who traditionally followed the seasons, moving south in the summer to graze their cattle. In recent years, climate change had turned traditional grazing lands to desert, and they'd ventured into the bread-basket of the

Middle Belt, encroaching on long-settled farmland and destroying crops. The Boko Haram insurgency in the North, another factor in the Fulani displacement, had led to a boom in the illegal weapons trade, and groups of herders often came heavily armed. Many of the massacres were reported to have been tit-for-tat disputes between the farmers and herders which had quickly escalated to brutal armed invasions by the herders. The government's failure to prevent the massacres or prosecute the killers, was not, according to some, merely a sign of their weakness. The attacks, according to a statement by a local chapter of the Christian Association of Nigeria, were a genocidal land grab by northern Muslims, to which the largely northern leadership of the Armed Forces and President Buhari, a Fulani Muslim by background, turned a blind eye. This version of events was, of course, vehemently rejected by Buhari, as well as his Yoruba vice-president, Yemi Osinbajo, who was also the pastor of a Lagos branch of the Redeemed Christian Church of God.

Pastor Isaac agreed that a strong secular national identity was essential for Nigeria. The country could not survive, he said, if any one group imposed its beliefs on another. 'The only way we can move forward,' he said, 'is to create a constitution which is not lop-sided, and which gives space for every other culture or religion to find expression.' But there is a great imbalance, he said, that first needs to be corrected. 'Islam is a political religion,' said Pastor Isaac. 'Christians are now waking up to the fact that Christianity is also a political religion.'

When a recording came to an end, I'd take off my headphones and take in the sounds of the night in Fawley. Despite the stillness of lockdown, it was never silent here. The hum of the refinery could be heard for miles around, like the buzzing of a giant fridge-freezer. For a time, both my grandfathers had worked at the refinery: one as a security guard, the other as a technical drawer. My parents had both grown up in this area, having sailing and dance classes at clubs funded by the oil company. It was strange to think that they'd all been serenaded by this same unbroken hum.

Some nights, the sound was joined by a rasping, engine-like overtone. My dad had told me that it came from the on-board generators of the tankers that docked at the offshore marine terminal.

Looking out from the shoreline at Ashlett Creek at night, the marine terminal formed a grid of glittering lights against the darkness of the sea. It was a kilometre and a half long, with up to eight oil tankers docking at any time, adding up to 2,000 each year, bringing a total of 22 million tonnes of crude oil to be processed. The oil was transformed into an array of products: gas, petrol, marine fuel, lubricants and plastics. Through direct underground pipelines, the refinery fuelled the planes of both Gatwick and Heathrow. Most of the cars on UK roads, according to the refinery's brochure, had tires containing Fawley-made artificial rubber. Where did the oil come from? Until I lived here, it had never occurred to me to ask. The answers were not surprising: the North Sea, Russia, South America, and West Africa.

When large oil reserves were first discovered in the Niger Delta in 1958, the refinery at Fawley was already seven years old. What had this constant flow of exported crude given in return? To the Delta itself, it had brought great degradation – each year, an estimated 22 million litres leaked into the wild. The pollution made subsistence farming and fishing impossible, forcing people to flee to the cities or turn to ever more perilous ways of surviving, like the illegal makeshift oil refineries that were themselves responsible for many of the leaks. To the wider country, the trade had brought all the volatile mixed blessings of a petrostate – the booms, the busts, the largesse and the self-serving corruption.

Here, the slow and stately movement of oil tankers up and down the Solent seemed as natural and ineluctable as the movements of the tide. For seventy years, the flow of crude had brought apprenticeships, jobs-for-life, and a prosperity so modest and mundane as to seem timeless, inevitable. The plant boxes in the village square, sponsored by ExxonMobil, full of fuchsias and geraniums. The garden gnomes, the caravans in the driveways. And in the harbour of the sailing club at Ashlett Creek, the rows of small leisure craft with self-deprecating names: Lapse of Reason, Ship for Brains.

On certain summer nights the sound from the refinery seemed much closer. The rising heat from the cooling ground after sunset would, according to my dad, form a kind of dome in the air, bending the soundwaves back down. The ambient hum became an air-shaking drone, like a jet plane perpetually just about to land. One evening, the soundwaves thickening the air as I walked, I wondered what it was I dreaded most. That the hum would just keep going: insatiable, world-devouring. Or that it would one day come to a stop.

I wandered under streetlights around the crescents and cul de sacs beyond the village shops. This part of Fawley was new to me. It was a 1960s redbrick estate, originally built for workers at the refinery. A mixture of terraced and semi-detached, the homes seemed spacious, pleasant, well-maintained. The gardens were a decent size, backing onto the modesty screen of forest that lay beyond the refinery's perimeter fence.

I'd always had a problem with domesticity. It often frustrated my wife: my obliviousness to my surroundings, my fidgety impatience around paint swatches, furniture showrooms, conversations about mortgages. I'd always vaguely disdained this side of life in favour of something more vital, though I no longer had much idea what that was. I could tell myself that what I found aversive was the consumerist complacency of it all. I knew that at the heart of the matter was a kind of restlessness. I was intolerant of modest visions, the mundane labours of stewardship, the simple pleasures of colour schemes. These days, though, something had changed.

Walking these streets, seeing the windows lit up with the glow of TVs, my desire for property was almost a physical pain. This was all I wanted. To be a family in a house like this, with a decent lawn, maybe a vegetable patch, a car in the drive and a trampoline in the back. To live a quiet and dignified life: uninteresting, untroubled by history.

¶ A couple of days before I arrived in Nigeria, my host Desmond Majekodunmi sent me an email asking if I would be a guest on his environment-themed radio show, *Earth Hour*, to discuss climate change and the media from my perspective as a journalist. I put off replying. Desmond had been so generous to me that I couldn't say no straight away. A conservationist and environmental activist from a prominent Lagos family, he'd agreed to accommodate me for the duration of my stay in Nigeria. In the same email, he told me that he'd lend me the services of his driver, Joseph, for the week, and that he had asked two of his contacts to accompany me to Redemption Camp, the town-sized Pentecostal complex built by the Redeemed Christian Church of God located between Lagos and Ibadan.

Joseph picked me up at the airport, and dropped me off at Desmond's house in Lekki, where he waited for me in his living room. Desmond was in his sixties, with a neat white goatee and a warm, wry manner. Early in our discussion about my stay, I mentioned apologetically that I might not be the most appropriate guest for his radio show. Firstly, I knew nothing much about climate change. And secondly, I wasn't a journalist. I could see where the misunderstanding might have come from: our mutual acquaintance, who'd introduced me to Desmond, was an esteemed reporter. I was an essayist, I told him. I didn't do this for a living. Desmond was undaunted. 'An essayist,' he said. 'I like it! I'll mention that in my introduction.' He wasn't really having me on his show for my expertise, he said. It was more for my accent. He promised to send me some articles about the recent IPCC report that I could read in the evening. I'll take the lead, he said. You'll be fine.

Born in the 50s, Desmond had spent the 70s and 80s

working in the music industry – 'the first black sound engineer in London,' he told me. He'd recorded LPs for Deep Purple, almost joined Thin Lizzy, rubbed shoulders with Fela Kuti, Mick Jagger and Marvin Gaye. It was on a trip to Kenya in the mid-1980s that his passion for the environment had taken hold. He'd made an ecological funk record in the late eighties with his then-wife Sheila, a well-known singer. They'd walked away from a record deal with Virgin, he said, because the executives had wanted them to dilute the environmental message. I'd later found some songs online. Sheila's Sade-like voice floated over delay-drenched dub beats, as Desmond dropped spoken-word paeans to mother nature and biodiversity: *The wetlands purify the water we need, provide a place for the fish to breathe!* Desmond appeared regularly in the media, talking about climate change, pollution and environmental protections. He had transformed a plot of inherited farmland into a nature park. He regularly met with religious leaders to raise awareness about global warming and protecting the environment.

That evening in Lagos, sitting on the bed under the ceiling fan of the guest room, I opened the articles on my laptop. I knew something about climate change, of course. I thought about it every day. Or rather, I tried not to. It was the fear that stalked me on every early-hours toilet trip, every unseasonably warm picnic, every bedtime story with L in which animals wandered idyllic landscapes, unafflicted by fire or flood. Since L had been born, I'd avoided reading articles on the topic. Nothing made it harder to focus on the demands and delights of the present with her than considering the future she would face. Now there was no escaping it.

I looked at the graphs tracing temperatures and CO_2 emissions from the industrial revolution to the present day: the lines rising and rising towards some cataclysm around the corner. I read the predictions: the famines, energy crises, civil wars that were inevitable; the still grimmer prospects in the absence of decisive global action. This was the most vital, unignorable truth we faced as a species. I believed it entirely, and it made me so tired. The narrative had all the urgency of the revivalist End Times vision, but without the sense of agency and excitement. Outside, beyond the mosquito mesh of the open window, crickets sang. In the heat, my focus began to flag, and I fell asleep. The next morning, I drove to the studio with Desmond, and he greeted his colleagues as we passed through the metal detector and up the stairs to the studio.

Desmond seemed to me an unlikely champion of Pentecostalism. He was well-read, worldly, cosmopolitan. His environmental activism was an interfaith affair – he met with Muslim clerics and traditional tribal leaders as well as priests and pastors. He spoke more of ecosystems and equilibrium than dark principalities and righteous dominion. He'd been raised a Christian, he said, and had explored many other belief systems in his lifetime, but in recent years had found himself coming full circle. Pentecostal churches, he said, had done great things for Nigeria. There were some charlatans, of course. But in a country that had faced such hardship and inequality, these churches had given people – particularly young people – hope, purpose, practical support.

I recalled little of our on-air conversation, which had the virtue, at least, of coming quickly to an end. What stayed with me was Desmond's opening monologue, which he delivered over a lush musical backing track. He didn't speak of God, but there was something of the church in his lyricism. It was, in part, a mournful jeremiad against inaction: the gravity of what faced us if we didn't turn things around. More than that it was an invocation of love. He praised the biosphere, its abundance and diversity. He spoke of our role as stewards of the world and all its riches, which could sustain us if only we honoured its limits.

We arrived at the central auditorium of Redemption Camp at around 10 o'clock at night. It took several minutes in the car to traverse the 1.5-kilometre length of the building. We walked through the gloom of the empty car park towards the blinding lights of the open hall. Inside, the high corrugated iron ceiling stretched back almost to a vanishing point, its repeating rows of pillars and metal vaults recalling the sturdy functionality of a train station. Underneath, there was a sea of off-white plastic chairs. Nearly all were empty, but towards the front, a few people were lying awkwardly across facing seats, attempting to sleep under the lights. It was the night before the opening night of the Holy Ghost Congress, the biggest event in the RCCG calendar, in which the camp would host hundreds of thousands of Redeemed members from branches around the world.

As we approached the front of the hall, the first thing I noticed were the bodies. About a dozen people lay sprawled on the white tiled expanse before the raised semi-circular stage. Some lay prostrate, others face up with arms outstretched, others on all fours. It took a second to register that this was a scene not of catastrophe but of intercession. One man kneeled up against the high wall of the stage, pressing his face and body against the red and gold fabric draped over it. How far had these people travelled? What was it they had brought to the altar with them?

We didn't hang around long. I felt slightly ashamed to be trespassing on such intimacy. Besides the murmur of prayer, the loudest sound in the hall was our footsteps. Occasionally a sharper sound broke through – a cough, the scraping of a chair – and I could hear the echo traverse the length of the vaulted ceiling, like the ricochet of a pebble down a well.

Before my trip, I'd watched a YouTube video showing drone footage of the Redemption Camp, the 2500-hectare site on the road to Ibadan that had transformed over the years into a kind of self-contained Pentecostal city. When the roof of an auditorium first came into view, to the left of the big wheel and carousel of the camp's amusement park, it appeared for a moment as an indeterminate brown expanse, too vast for the eye to register as a building. As soon as the vision resolved, the camera swivelled right to take in a far larger building. It looked identical to the first, but its metal roof extended so implausibly far and wide that it resembled a crude photoshop job come to life, or the endless repeated patterns of a hallucination. This was the first auditorium we'd visit: the smaller one was now used as a centre for children's activities. Already this larger hall had been dwarfed by a new auditorium, not shown on the video, which looked out over the rest of Redemption Camp from the top of a hill.

I was drawn to the RCCG because it seemed in many ways antithetical to SCOAN, despite the surface commonalities: the Pentecostal style, the Yoruba roots, the international renown. If SCOAN thrust skywards, dynamic and unstable, fuelled by individual hope and desperation, the RCCG seemed more sturdy: all steady, horizontal spread. If TB Joshua was the logical endpoint of an imported Ayn Randian hyper-individualist

224

Christianity, perhaps the RCCG represented the triumph of a different impulse: a spirit of self-sustaining collectivism whose absence was notable in the late-capitalist West.

I'd been reading a pdf of a RCCG manual for workers-in-training, written by the General Overseer, E. A. Adeboye. It was a sober document, full of diagrams of branching management structures, and bullet-pointed lists outlining the duties of the key roles within the church, backed up with verses from the New Testament. In its uniting of the visionary with the practical, the gifts of the spirit with the mundane exigencies of church life, it put flesh on the bones of Paul's teaching that the church should act as a single body.

Adeboye listed the qualities needed for each kind of worker. The ushers' material contentment and ethical rigour, to guard against the temptation to steal from the collection pots they passed around. The prayer warriors' passion and love of privacy, to sustain them in their hours cloistered in a hidden prayer room as the public meetings took place. The sanitation workers' cleanliness, lowly servant spirit, and high tolerance for nauseating sights and smells. Humility, wrote Adeboye, was a quality that every worker should share. Each one, from pastor to deacon, from chorister to cleaner, should 'surrender one's self as an instrument of God'. 'No department is superior to another,' he wrote, 'and none can perform at the exclusion of the other. All of them are complimentary and mutually supportive.'

In David Sloan Wilson's writing about superorganisms, he often referred to a Nobel Prize-winning political scientist called Elinor Ostrom. She was interested in what the ecologist Garrett Hardin dubbed the 'Tragedy of the Commons': the trap by which behaviour that is rational at the individual level – someone grazing a few

225

extra sheep on the common land – leads to collective ruin when everybody acts the same way. She'd studied groups of fishermen in Turkey and Canada and irrigation-dependent farmers in the Philippines, Japan and elsewhere in an attempt to understand what determined their respective success or failure at averting conflict or the depletion of resources. She identified eight 'design principles': features that the successful groups shared. Her ideas were cited by business consultants, but also by left-wing activists and ecologists. The fishermen and farmers of her study had succeeded – with their bottom-up systems of cooperation – at solving a local problem that we as a species were far from figuring out at larger scales.

I wondered, flicking through the workers-in-training manual, whether E. A. Adeboye had read Ostrom too. Most of her 'design principles' were apparent. He talked about the balance between giving and taking: members were expected to faithfully tithe – those who gave less than their share would not get to heaven – but those who were bereaved or financially destitute were offered support. He talked about graded sanctions for rule-breakers, and the system of appeal for those who felt unjustly punished. He talked about the tiered nature of the church structure, and the balance it struck between centralized authority and local autonomy.

Perhaps the principle at which the church most excelled was the first, seemingly obvious item on Ostrom's list. A group, she said, must have clearly defined boundaries. This was not simply about knowing who's in or out. 'You know that you're part of a group,' writes Sloan Wilson, summarizing the condition, 'and you know what that group is about.'

There could be few groups with a surer sense of their own purpose than the RCCG. The guide opens with a summary of the church's mission statement, one that I heard repeated almost word-for-word from many of the RCCG supporters I spoke to.

1. To make Heaven.
2. To take as many people as possible with us.
3. To have a member of the Redeemed Christian Church of God in every family of all nations.
4. To accomplish No. 1 above, holiness will be our lifestyle.
5. To accomplish Nos. 2 & 3 above, we will plant churches within five minutes' walking distance in every city and town of developing countries and within five minutes driving distance in every city and town of developed countries.

The appeal of the mission statement was partly in its snappy formulation: those first two lines had the zing of an advertising slogan. Its genius was in its synthesis of a wildly ambitious, inexhaustible goal with the most concrete and quotidian: the individual pursuit of holiness, and the growth of the social body, one church at a time. The elusive finish line was always on the horizon, and the next step was always sharply in focus.

In 1980, the ailing founder of the RCCG, Reverend Josiah Akindayomi, appointed a young pastor called E. A. Adeboye as his successor. When Akindayomi died later that year, the church had just thirty-nine branches, all in the south-west of Nigeria. In the four decades since E. A. Adeboye took over, the church has gained over 7000 branches in Nigeria alone, and thousands more in eighty countries around the world.

Before he was a full-time pastor, E. A. Adeboye was a lecturer in Lagos University, having gained a PhD in Mathematics. The church's expansion was helped, no doubt, by his head for maths. Judging from the mission statement, which was brought in under his leadership, he had an equal mastery of language. He understood that the vision of the RCCG was not merely an end but a tool. Just as the mop was the cleaner's tool, and the collection bowl the usher's, the church's vision was a social tool for strengthening the bonds by which the usher, the cleaner and every other member could work together for common ends.

If it could have been viewed from a height, the expansion of the church would have looked a lot like life itself. Whenever a local branch reached a certain size, its congregation divided, like a single embryonic cell becoming two, or a beehive swarming when a new queen emerges and half the colony leaves with her, the scouts venturing out ahead in search of a new home .

I spent the first day at Redemption Camp writing down numbers in my notebook then staring at them, stumped by the maths, wondering if they were wild exaggerations or just really, really large. Walking around the 1.5-kilometre auditorium, I was told that at full capacity, it held four million people. We drove to the National Kitchen, the main catering centre for the camp, where under a hangar-like roof, rows and rows of cauldrons sizzled with oil as chunks of beef were fried by the wheelbarrow-load. In the next door building, at least 300 cows were slaughtered daily. The kitchen, we were told, could feed three million people a day. Meals were free, but a VIP menu featuring 'continental' cuisine – presumably from a continent other than Africa – was available for a fee. We drove to the camp's maternity clinic. An administrator called Precious told me that in a typical week-long event like the Holy Ghost Congress, around a hundred

228

women would usually give birth. It was late morning on the first day, and most attendees had yet to arrive. Four babies had already been delivered today.

We drove up the hill towards the 3-by-3 kilometre auditorium, which lay behind a large complex of office buildings. This, I had read, accommodated 12 million people. I walked down the aisle of the auditorium with Pastor Chidi, a friend of Desmond's who'd accompanied me as a guide. Beneath the iron rafters of the high ceiling, the grimy white plastic chairs were covered with a layer of red-grey dust. Like the other auditorium, the building lacked walls. The place was not opulent, but neither was it austere. As we reached the stage, we saw draped fabrics, fairy lights, Christmas trees, potted ferns. The decorations reminded me, vast scale notwithstanding, of a Christmas party in a village hall. 'Adeboye believes in a church without walls,' Pastor Chidi said. 'If you have a church building that is fixed, permanent, walled, it is harder to expand. Church is not the building, but the souls that gather there.'

Pastor Chidi told me about a time, in this new auditorium, when Adeboye, commonly known as Daddy G.O., had addressed the witches and wizards in the audience. He told them to come up to the altar. 'If you don't,' he said, 'you will die within seven days.' One by one, people stood up. The altar area slowly filled with people. Some of the congregation cursed those that walked forward. Daddy G.O. rebuked them, and praised the witches and wizards for answering the call.

Partway through my first day at Redemption Camp, I felt overcome with a paralyzing incuriosity. My companions, Pastor Chidi and a barrister called Funmi, were diligently playing their roles as fixers – texting contacts, trying to procure interviews with pastors and other church figures. I, in turn, felt obliged to act like a journalist. But I didn't want to talk to another Pentecostal. I didn't want to sit through another sermon. I didn't want to hear from anyone else about how humble Daddy G.O. was. I could no longer reciprocate the hallelujah expressions of the people telling me that this expanse of concrete and plastic seating used to be virgin forest.

I'd wanted the RCCG to be the anti-SCOAN, to redeem Nigerian Pentecostalism for me, but the vitality and abundance of the camp suddenly resembled that of a monocrop, stretching endlessly and uniformly across the landscape. It was difficult to ignore that RCCG's emphasis on mutual care and stewardship existed within a capitalist creed of infinite expansion. The Redemption Camp was an international centre of commerce, a testament to the church's courting of corporate power and the super-rich. There were luxury villas for sale. Nivea, Coca Cola, Procter and Gamble and Unilever were among the corporations whose adverts and trade stands helped fund the gatherings at the camps.

In one RCCG programme brochure, quoted in Asonzeh Ukah's PhD thesis on the church, the company Unilever placed an advert whose slogan rewrote a Bible verse for the purposes of selling detergent. 'For sin shall not have dominion over you,' wrote Paul in his letter to the Romans. 'For you are not under the law, but under grace.' Over a picture of a box of OMO Multi Action Super Stain Remover, the words were placed in quotation marks: 'Neither sin nor stain will have dominion over you.'

A hundred and fifty years ago, the territory on which Redemption Camp is located was ruled by the Royal Niger Company, a British trading company backed by a mercenary army, who exported palm oil, imposed a monopoly on trade, and violently suppressed local tribes who defied it. The company, which prompted the formation of colonial Nigeria when it sold its terrain to the British state in 1900, would later be bought by Lever Brothers, which in turn would become Unilever. Even now, the spread of Christianity in Nigeria was not untainted with commercial interests. Some stains were more stubborn than others.

But who was I, a suburban Brit weaned on petrol and palm oil, to find fault? This place was a functioning ecosystem within a fractured, dysfunctional state. It had its own public transport system, school, health system, police force, 25-megawatt gas-fuelled power station. How could I appreciate the achievement of the RCCG without tasting the difficulties of life outside: the rubbish, the crime, the traffic, the reliance on generators?

The sociologist J. D. Y. Peel, in his introduction to Asonzeh Ukah's book about the Redeemed Church, suggested that the likes of E. A. Adeboye carried the baton of Nigerian nationalism that politicians had dropped. 'It is as if it is saying to the state: "This is the way to carry out the nationalist project of development!"' he writes. 'More than that, the faith in Nigeria's high destiny as a nation, a beacon to the rest of Africa, still continues but is displaced onto the RCCG, working on and through Nigeria.'

It would be wrong to dismiss the RCCG as purveyors of an imported Western Christianity. The doctrine of the RCCG is the product of a relationship that stretches back almost a century, a two-step dance between the embrace of Western influence and the assertion of African identity, between a worldview grounded in the local and a more universal vision, charged with the vitality of a prosperous *elsewhere*.

231

Its founder, Josiah Akindayomi, born in 1905, began his career as a *babalowo* and herbalist, before seeking education at an Anglican Church Mission School, where he converted to Christianity. He left the Anglican church for the Cherubim and Seraphim, a Nigerian church that had make a break from colonial Christianity with its focus on healing and syncretic ritual. Along with a group of followers, he split from the Cherubim and Seraphim to form his own church, in which he disavowed traditional practices like polygamy and consulting the dead, and forged links with Pentecostal ministries from South Africa and the US, which were severed after Nigeria gained independence in 1960.

Akindayomi's successor has danced a similar dialectic. While absorbing some of the doctrine and style of American neo-Pentecostals, Adeboye has also imbued worship meetings with revived Yoruba traditions, such as the lengthy performances of *ewi*, in which Adeboye, echoed by backing singers arranged in circles, praises the God of Abraham in ecstatic verse whose form predates by many years the arrival of Christianity in Nigeria.

At the time I was revisiting the recordings from my Lagos trip, I was reading *Pentecostal Republic* by the Nigerian sociologist Ebenezer Obadare. He opens the book with an anecdote about Reuben Abati, a veteran journalist and newspaper columnist well-known for his searing critiques of political corruption. Abati surprised his readers in 2011 when he took a job as a special advisor and spokesperson for President Goodluck Jonathan, whose administration he'd often criticized in his column. Over the next five years, he stepped up to the role, pugnaciously defending the president and attacking his perceived enemies. By the time he left the job in 2016, he'd lost much of

232

his credibility as political commentator. In October 2016, an article he wrote for the Lagos *Guardian* provoked a storm of debate in the press and social media.

In the piece, Abati claimed that Aso Villa, the seat of the Nigerian presidency, was under siege by demonic forces. It was a place, he said, where 'most people... always bathed in the morning with blood. Goat blood. Ram blood. Whatever animal blood.'

'When presidents make mistakes,' he continued, 'they are probably victims of a force higher than what we can imagine. Every student of Aso Villa politics would readily admit that when people get in there, they actually become something else. They act like they are under a spell. We need to rescue Nigeria from the forces of darkness. Aso Villa should be converted into a spiritual museum, and abandoned.'

It was not just the grand guignol narrative of Abati's essay that was remarkable, but the sympathetic response with which the majority of commentators and politicians received it. Some, like Femi Adesina, a special adviser to President Buhari at the time, argued that Abati's fatalism was unhelpful. Along with other senior political figures like Femi Fani-Kayode and Sina Kawonise, he nonetheless assented to Abati's basic claim: that in the arena of Nigerian politics, as well as daily life, demons and roving spirits had as much agency as any human figure.

The ubiquity of this worldview, argued Obadare, was an unfortunate side-effect of the Pentecostal boom. The election of Obasanjo in 1999, known as the 'born-again president', ushered in an era in which megapastors like Adeboye have played an outsized role in shaping the political imagination of both the general public and the political elite.

The spiritual warfare narrative, wrote Obadare, was

convenient for politicians keen to evade responsibility for their mistakes or misdemeanours: if spirits called the shots, why the need for individual human accountability? It also meant that facts and empiricism could be discarded. One only need claim authority through 'spiritual intelligence' or prophetic words. All this risked a catastrophic breakdown in the fabric of civil society, as the consensus reality between political opponents got smaller and smaller. Why debate or compromise with someone you claim is possessed by diabolical forces?

While I was in Fawley reading *Pentecostal Republic*, the televangelist Paula White was working for the Trump administration, and horrified liberals on my Facebook feed were sharing videos of her defiantly striding across the stage, exorcising demons with a blood-curdling scream. 'We cancel every surprise from witchcraft in the marine kingdom,' she said. 'Any hex, any spells, any witchcraft, we curse it, we break it!' The imported Bible-Belt demonology that for so long had occupied Nigerian politics had loudly announced its arrival in Washington DC. Strangely enough, it seemed to have picked up marine spirits from the Niger Delta along the way.

In March 2020, Rodney Howard-Browne, one of the central figures in the Toronto Blessing, had announced to his Florida congregation that coronavirus was a lie, part of a satanic plot by globalists to force people to take vaccines that would kill them. He defied the lockdown, encouraging his congregation to continue shaking hands, because 'we're raising up revivalists, not pansies.'

A week after the US election, a comment from an old Immanuel friend called James turned up on my Facebook feed. He was debating with American evangelicals on the public posts of a husband-and-wife televangelist duo named Johnny and Elizabeth Enlow. Johnny Enlow had written a long post about the 'stolen' election. The period of confusion, he said, was God's way of separating the true Republicans from the 'Republicans in Name Only', and the true seekers of the Kingdom of God from the 'Kingdom in Name Only'. 'The real question is are you a "loyalist" or a patriot?' he wrote. 'One takes some cowardice. One takes some courage. CHOOSE!'

James got in with the first comment to point out mildly that there hadn't yet been any evidence offered to back up the charges of electoral fraud. Little discussion ensued. The question of what precisely had happened appeared unimportant. Below, hundreds of people left emoji-laden affirmations of loyalty, full of hallelujahs. The upheaval, many wrote, was a sign that God was moving, that revival was around the corner. One woman quoted a song by Delirious, the English worship band whom the Immanuel youth would go to see when they did their monthly worship concerts in Southampton. 'Dancers will dance upon injustice!' she wrote, noting that the song 'Did You Feel the Mountains Tremble?' had been made an anti-lockdown anthem by the US worship leader Sean Feucht, who'd done a nationwide tour earlier in the year, in defiance of restrictions.

I was struck not so much by the unhinged anger of the original post, but the sheer joy in the comments. How sweet it must have been to survey the scenes across the world – pandemic, wildfire, civil unrest – and feel not dread but anticipation. To see not suffering and precarity but the glory ahead.

'The best lack all conviction, while the worst / Are full of passionate intensity.' Those lines from the Second Coming seemed more apt each time I thought of them. Yet the mixture of despair and self-congratulation annoyed me, not least because I recognized myself in it. What good was a rationalism that dismantled myths, illuminated endless nuance, and bred paralysis?

I spoke to Desmond over the phone in April 2021. We did the customary post-covid catch-up. He was double-jabbed and doing well. His church, The House on the Rock, still mostly met remotely. Nigeria had so far not fared as badly as many other countries, although the lack of social safety net and large informal sector made lock-downs difficult to enforce. The fall in the price of oil had impacted the economy: in Lagos, the number of those going hungry had doubled.

These were times, Desmond said, of trial and trib-ulation. Dark forces were rising in Nigeria, he said. Besides violence in the north and Middle Belt, there had been a rise in witchcraft-related killings closer to home. He sent me a video of a man who'd been caught and arrested, and who explained on camera that he'd killed a young girl to sell her organs as fetish objects. Her corpse lay beside him, covered in a black plastic sheet. Someone held a glass jar up to the camera, asking the man to identify the contents. 'The sense organs,' he said. 'Eyes, nose, skin.'

This year, two more RCCG ministers had been elect-ed to high positions in government. The pastor of the House on the Rock, Paul Adefarasin, had made headlines for bringing politics to the pulpit. A video of his sermon had gone viral on social media, apparently reaching the ears of the government and US state department. The sermon began to make sense of the odd group of adopted forefathers – American industrialists, Anglican bishops, pan-African nationalists – that I'd seen on the walls of his church. The video was a clear political intervention, a shot

236

across the bows. He railed against corrupt politicians and bemoaned Nigeria's poverty and lack of industrialization in language that was impassioned and self-consciously statesmanlike, at times technocratic. What kept the country from progressing, he said, was the unbalanced constitution. He issued a challenge for the victors of the 2023 election. 'The next administration,' he said, 'should not be allowed to access power unless they provide a constitution which reflects "we the people"... Nigerians, wake up!' he said. 'It's worth dying for.'

Desmond had persisted with his environmental activism. He'd continued speaking to religious leaders, trying to get them to take climate change seriously. Already, the changes in weather were becoming unignorable. Some pastors were receptive, but others were dismissive. Some recognized the importance of the issue, but questioned why it should be on Nigerians to combat climate change. They'd already suffered disproportionately from the side-effects of the fossil fuel industry. It was the industrialized West who'd enjoyed the benefits, and who should foot the bill for fixing the problem.

For some Pentecostal leaders, Desmond said, the urgent calls to avert disaster seemed irrelevant. Why be distracted by the conservation of the physical world, when Jesus was coming back?

The Redeemed Christian Church of God's End Times vision was not unusual among Pentecostals. The rapture, they believed, would see believers ascend to heaven, while an elite resistance force, known as the Tribulation Saints, would stay behind to resist the antichrist. Christ would return with his bride to pass judgement on sinners and usher in a 1000-year reign of peace. After this, the material world would be abolished. As sinners faced eternal torment, a new heaven and a new earth would

237

be created. It would be the end of all imperfection, all impermanence.

We arrived in the old auditorium just as the opening night's service was beginning. An usher showed us to our place in the front row of the hall. The white tiled floor stretched before us. Beyond it, on the raised stage, the worship band was starting up.

My first concern, as the song got going and the crowd around me began to move, was what to do with my hands. On the giant screen in front of us, I saw myself at the front and centre of one of the cycling shots of the crowd. It wasn't just my colour and lack of rhythm – this point of pale stiffness in a mass of swaying bodies and brown skin – that marked me out. I radiated agnosticism. It was insufficient, I realized, to simply sway to the music, hands in my pockets or at my side. But I could not in good faith raise my hands above my head. The least bad option, I decided, was to clap along. I would endorse the rhythms, at least, while remaining theologically non-aligned.

I'm not sure exactly when it was that I began to cry. Probably around the time of the fourth song, when the prosaic rhythms became more complex, and the drummer, bassist and two percussionists – one on the Yoruban talking drum – locked into a groove. I'd heard of the symbiosis between the Lagos music scene and the Pentecostal churches, and this seemed to be evidence: the music was really, really good. The lead vocalist was calling out lines and his back-up singers – a dozen men and women in radiant blue waistcoats and dresses – were calling back in harmony. It was as if the praise and worship of my youth had disguised itself as Fela Kuti to pass through my defences. It had swapped the acoustic jangle for the clean bright lines of electric guitar, the plodding 4/4 beat for playful mutating polyrhythms, before hitting me with the words that were no less penetrating for all the years I'd deflected them: Lord and Majesty. Hallowed be your name. You are worthy to be praised. I dabbed my eyes with a tissue and tried to think of profane things. The last thing I needed was to break down in front of the cameras, to have hands laid on me, to be the prodigal *oyinbo* at the altar call, to satisfy my companions' irritating missionary zeal.

A couple of dull and grating Anglican hymns offered some respite. Then the choir – around two hundred singers on a tiered stand to the right of the stage – began to sing a praise song in Yoruba. It was a mid-tempo song, all winding guitar melodies and glassy electric piano, with a swaying, syncopated rhythm that was at once propulsive and consoling. The women wore gold head wraps, white shirts and gold skirts, the men white shirts and gold ties. They gathered three to a microphone and danced as they sang. A young woman led the song, standing at the front, also wearing gold and white. She sang each verse like a storyteller, her voice powerful, her face animated, as if she was surprising herself with each unfolding line. The choir repeated her verse in full, raising their arms, as she echoed, embellished, and played in-between the lines.

Later in the evening, I would be reassuringly unmoved by the sermons, impressed but not overcome by E. A. Adeboye's gentle gravitas. But my doubt and indifference were powerless against the singing.

It was the way that every chorister seemed at once extravagantly free and entirely subsumed to the song. The singers' movements were not coordinated. Each one danced alone, as if caught in their own private reverie. To behold them together was to see a common pulse, a single forcefield animating them, a shimmering murmuration in white and gold.

Perhaps this was not so different from what the Winfields had felt on their first visit to SCOAN, 50 kilometres down the road, some twenty years ago. When Susan and Gavin had pitched their SCOAN visits as a faith-building antidote to the cynicism and unbelief of the West, they were articulating the great folly of God-chasing revivalism. They were also naming an undeniable truth.

I'd never been in a room with so much faith in it. Like a hut-dwelling English peasant dumbstruck by the stained-glass grandeur of a cathedral, what undid me was the contrast between the strained, uncertain muddle of my everyday life and this monumental collective joy. The vast yes of the congregation proved nothing, allayed no misgivings, and it had blown my heart right open.

Was the power of this moment in its otherness? The unfamiliar melodies, the round Yoruba vowels, the great distances and unfathomable crowd? It was, perhaps, the more familiar strangeness that the otherness recalled. Sunday mornings at Immanuel in the years before I understood the words. Before the propositions and the doubts, when all of faith was in the cadences, the rising and resolving chords, the outstretched hands and dustmotes moving through the light.

As the song ended, a saxophone player walked out onto the stage. Over lush synth strings, he played an ornate, reverb-laden version of Great is Thy Faithfulness. Partway through, Pastor Chidi leaned over to tell me this was Kunle Ajayi, Pastor E. A. Adeboye's personal saxophonist. Whenever Adeboye was about to address the congregation, Ajayi would emerge and play a kind of fanfare. The song finished. The General Overseer appeared, stepped up to the pulpit, then lowered himself to his knees in prayer.

EPILOGUE

On the second day of TB Joshua's funeral at the Synagogue Church, his disciples took to the stage. A microphone was passed around as sixty-four disciples introduced themselves by name and nationality. They came from sixteen different countries, among them Mexico, Colombia and Indonesia, as well as the US and the UK. Some seemed barely out of their teens; others were in late middle-age. A senior Nigerian disciple named Anne, recently promoted to prophetess, began her tribute. 'How to describe,' she said, 'someone so indescribable? How to define someone so indefinable? Human and divine?'

TB Joshua had died on 5 June 2021, days away from his 58th birthday. According to news reports, he'd left the auditorium of his church partway through a Saturday service, apparently to rest in his room. When he failed to emerge, one of his disciples had entered and found him collapsed. He was pronounced dead later that night. The news spread throughout the morning on social media, before the Synagogue Church of All Nations made an official announcement. 'God has taken His servant Prophet TB Joshua home,' the statement read, 'as it should be by divine will.' Over a month later, his funeral underway, there had been no mention of a cause of death.

In the days that followed the news, I'd felt oddly unmoored. It was like nothing I'd known before: no grief, but all the disorientation of a bereavement. The fresh double-take each morning, the small astonishment of every verb pulled into the past tense. It was hard to believe he was really dead.

I reached out to old friends and interviewees: Giles, Mary, Dan and Kate. I asked Dan and Kate what they thought would happen next. They told me they'd given up on speculating. At first, Dan had hoped that his parents and other two siblings, still devoted SCOAN supporters, would finally leave the church. With TB Joshua gone, he thought, the whole thing might quickly collapse. After Dan and Kate discussed the news with their counsellor, they sobered up. He urged caution. That's not how these things tend to end, he said.

Two days into the five-day funeral celebration, it was clear that this was not just a laying to rest but a statement of intent. The last disciple to speak was a blonde American woman in her thirties. 'Daddy, we will preserve your legacy, we will defend your legacy,' she said. 'One chapter in this remarkable journey may have come to an end, but it is not the end, never the end. Prophet TB Joshua lives on.'

In Teju Cole's novel, *Every Day is for the Thief*, a Nigerian returns to Lagos in the early 2000s, after years of living abroad. Sitting in an internet café, he catches a glimpse of his neighbour's screen. Realizing he is seated next to one of the email fraudsters for which Nigeria has become infamous, the narrator reflects on this form of storytelling that has become a means of survival for so many. 'I realize Lagos is a city of Scheherazades. The stories unfold in ever more fanciful iterations and, as in the myth, those who tell the best stories are richly rewarded.'

Amid the austerity and crisis of early-eighties Nigeria, Temitope Balogun Joshua, a young high-school drop-out from Ondo state, moved to Lagos and found work in a poultry farm. Not long afterwards, he began telling the story of prophethood that would eventually grant him riches, power and impunity. I'd always seen him as more of a sultan: a corrupt autocrat, indifferent to the trail of private miseries he left in his wake. But Joshua was

244

nothing if not a Scheherazade. Alongside his storyteller's gift – his instinct for the longings of his listeners, his ability to string them endlessly along – he had the anxiety of somebody forestalling death one tale at a time.

I only got a sense of this side of Joshua when I spoke to Mary Winfield. Disciples had learned, she said, that Joshua was never more volatile than when he was wrong. He prophesied that Hilary Clinton would win the US elections in 2016, and was widely derided on Nigerian social media when the results came in. When news of Trump's victory broke, the veteran disciples instinctively gave the prophet a wide berth. A new disciple, a young Egyptian man, approached Joshua to earnestly ask how he should respond to the critics mocking the prophecy on the Arabic SCOAN Facebook page. The disciple found himself on a plane back to Egypt the next day.

After the deadly collapse of the guesthouse, I was initially stunned by Joshua's response: the bizarre conspiracy theory, the messianic self-centredness. But what choice did he have? One side-effect of his claim of divine anointing was that it forced him to constantly outrun the facts of his ordinary humanity. To have even acknowledged the collapse as a tragedy would have risked a greater collapse in his reputation as Man of God. He could only up the ante, whatever the cost to truth or dignity. The collapse could either be proof of his human fallibility, or a Satanic attack that proved his anointing.

TB Joshua did not merely make a fortune from the story of prophethood he told. He built a vast and teetering human edifice around it, one that defied gravity for decades, held up by money and silence, and one that now faced a crisis in the wake of his death. He rose far above the poverty of his upbringing, but never left the precarity behind.

245

On the fourth day of the funeral, Joshua's body was brought from Prayer Mountain to the Synagogue Church for the lying in state. A motorcade of police vehicles and SUVs made its way through the dense crowd gathered outside the church, followed by a military marching band on the back of a lorry, then a hearse displaying Joshua's body. He was laid out in a full-length white gown, his head resting on a white pillow, giving a sense of peace and repose that was heightened by the clamour around him.

At the time of the funeral, the question of succession remained unclear. Joshua's wife, Evelyn, was named the head of the church immediately after his death. A few weeks later, the official SCOAN Facebook page released an interview with Joshua, purportedly conducted in the final weeks of his life. He stopped short of definitive statements, but appeared to suggest that Evelyn did not have his blessing as successor. 'The issue of family should not come into the issue of the church,' he said. SCOAN was an apostolic ministry, he added, not a business to be handed down. When asked what he'd done to prepare for succession, he pointed to the five senior disciples to whom he'd recently given the titles of prophet and prophetess. It was clear that the atmosphere of competition and mutual distrust that TB Joshua fostered in life would shape whatever came next.

In the following months, news reports would give glimpses of the drama unfolding within SCOAN. Many of the senior disciples, including the remaining Winfields, would be sent home. Evelyn Joshua, sidelined by her husband for years, would assert her authority over those who'd come to believe they were heirs to Joshua's anointing.

On the fifth day of the funeral, Joshua's mausoleum was revealed: a hangar-sized hall within the SCOAN complex, constructed with impressive speed. A pathway of illuminated posts marked the route that future visitors would tread, past a large circular fountain, its water lit up neon blue, towards the marble grave, housed within a white colonnade that held up a triangular roof, like a Greek temple in miniature.

SCOAN did everything possible to emphasize how his passing was neither untimely nor unforeseen. He was called home – and if he did not physically ascend to heaven, his death could at least remain perfectly vague, unblemished by details of bodily failure. Now the inconvenient fact of the mortal man was gone, TB Joshua had become pure mythology. All-too-fallible flesh had become word.

Acknowledgements

Special thanks to all the ex-Immanuelites and former SCOAN disciples I spoke to, as well as the friends and relatives of disciples, for your honesty and generosity, for lending me books and materials, for the contributions to the blog, and for the conversations over the years. I won't list you all, since it would be a jumble of pseudonyms and actual names. Particularly deep gratitude to my main interviewees. This book would be nothing without your stories and reflections; any errors of fact or judgement (ethical, artistic, theological) are entirely mine. To those Immanuelites who preferred not to talk, and those to whom I didn't reach out, for being part of this community which meant so much to me: I hope that my affection for Immanuel is apparent to you, even while our conclusions may differ.

To everyone else who shared with me their experiences of faith, doubt and ambivalence, and in doing so persuaded me this was a topic worth pursuing.

To the following friends for the comments on drafts, reading suggestions, grant application support, accountability sessions, and stimulating and restorative conversations: Duncan Mortimer, Emily Zaraa, Craig Rye, Matt West, Val Drayton, Peter Middleton, Nick Parton. To Ezra Anton Greene and Thomas Youngs, for the emails. To Adie Liddiard, Solveig Godauski and all at Sunday Assembly Southampton, for letting me try out a draft segment of the book in one of your services, and for the helpful discussions which followed.

To Abbie Fielding-Smith, for reading drafts and helping me with my trip to Lagos. To Michael Peel and Emily Witt for the advice and contacts. To Desmond Majekodunmi for the generous hospitality and insight. To all those who helped make my Lagos trip fruitful, particularly Pastor Isaac, Pastor Chidi and Barrister Funmi. To Nicholas Ibekwe and Joshua Craze, for the valuable information.

To all my colleagues at italk, and particularly to Vicky

Hammond, Clare Harvey and Amy Francis, for supporting my writing and indulging my requests for sabbaticals.

To Isabel Clarke for being a therapeutic inspiration, and for influencing my thinking around faith, collectivity and the self.

To the judges of the Fitzcarraldo Editions Essay Prize for giving the book a chance. To Jacques Testard for the advocacy, encouragement, excellent editing, practical support, and for being cool and unflappable when I felt anything but. To the whole Fitzcarraldo team, with special thanks to Joely Day and Clare Bogen. To David Wolf and the *Guardian* Long Read team. To all at *n+1* magazine. To Marco Roth, for the kindness, wise counsel, reading, editing and encouragement over the years. To Guy Robertson and all at Mahler & LeWitt Studios for an amazing residency in 2016. To Joanna Pocock for the solidarity and pep talk. To Arts Council England and the Robert Silvers Foundation for the financial support which enabled me to take time off work to write.

To the following writers and scholars, whose work helped shape this book in important ways: Tanya Luhrmann, David Sloan Wilson, Francis Spufford, Asonzeh Ukah, Ruth Marshall and Ebenezer Obadare.

To mum and dad for the years of conversations, the childcare, and the unstinting support throughout this project, whose spirit you understood even while its subject matter was painful for you. To all my siblings, particularly Ian, for the work on the blog, comments on drafts, and TB Joshua chats over the years, and Jon, my first reader, exposed to more messy half-formed drafts than anyone else, for the reassurance, generosity with time, great observations and ear for language.

To M, for the conversations, suggestions, patience, support, labour and love, without which this book would have been impossible to write, and to L, for the daily delights: I love you both so much.

Fitzcarraldo Editions
8-12 Creekside
London, SE8 3DX
United Kingdom

ISBN 978-1910695-67-8

Design by Ray O'Meara
Typeset in Fitzcarraldo
Printed and bound by TJ Books

fitzcarraldoeditions.com

Fitzcarraldo Editions